Race and the Constitution

From the Philadelphia Convention to the Age of Segregation

Other Titles in this Series:

Race and the Constitution

From the Philadelphia Convention to the Age of Segregation

by **Paul Finkelman**

**Published by the
American Historical Association
400 A Street, SE
Washington, D.C. 20003
www.historians.org**

PAUL FINKELMAN is the President William McKinley Distinguished Professor of Law and Public Policy and Senior Fellow Government Law Center at Albany Law School, in Albany, New York. He is the author of numerous scholarly articles and books, and is an expert in areas such as the law of slavery, religious liberty, constitutional law, and legal issues surrounding baseball. He was a Fellow in Law and the Humanities at Harvard Law School and received his Ph.D. and M.A. in history from the University of Chicago and his B.A. from Syracuse University. His scholarship has been cited by numerous courts including the United States Supreme Court.

Prior to his position at Albany Law School, Finkelman held endowed chairs at the University of Tulsa College of Law, University of Akron School of Law, and Cleveland-Marshall School of Law School. He held the Charlton W. Tebeau Chair in history at the University of Miami and also taught in the history departments at Virginia Tech, Washington University in St. Louis, and the University of Texas at Austin. In 2009 he gave the Nathan I. Huggins Lectures at W.E.B. DuBois Institute at Harvard University.

AHA EDITORS: Elisabeth Grant, Liz Townsend

LAYOUT: Chris Hale

The New Essays on American Constitutional History series is also sponsored by the Institute for Constitutional History at the New-York Historical Society and the George Washington University Law School.

© 2010 by the American Historical Association
ISBN: 978-0-87229-169-0

Published in 2010 by the American Historical Association. As publisher, the American Historical Association does not adopt official views on any field of history and does not necessarily agree or disagree with the views expressed in this book.

Library of Congress Cataloging-in-Publication Data:

Finkelman, Paul, 1949–

Race and the Constitution: from the Philadelphia Convention to the age of segregation / by Paul Finkelman. p. cm. -- (New essays on American constitutional history)

Includes bibliographical references.

ISBN 978-0-87229-169-0

1. African Americans--Legal status, laws, etc.—United States--History—19th century. 2. Slavery--Law and legislation--United States--History. 3. Constitutional history—United States. I. Title.

| KF4757F56 2010 | 342.7308'7--dc22 | 2010023704 |

Table of Contents

Series Introduction

New Essays on American Constitutional History is published by the American Historical Association, in association with the Institute for Constitutional Studies. This series follows the lead of its predecessor, the Bicentennial Essays on the Constitution, published by the AHA under the editorship of Herman Belz as part of the commemoration of the two hundredth anniversary of the Constitution over two decades ago. The goal remains the same. The essays are intended to provide both students and teachers with brief, accessible, and reliable introductions to some of the most important aspects of American constitutional development. The essays reflect the leading scholarship in the field and address topics that are classic, timely, and always important.

American constitutionalism is characterized by a series of tensions. Such tensions are persistent features of American constitutional history, and they make a frequent appearance in these essays. The American tradition emphasizes the importance of written constitutions. The United States Constitution declares that "this Constitution" is the "supreme law of the land." But time moves on. Politics and society are ever changing. How do we manage the tension between being faithful to a written constitutional text and adapting to changing political circumstances? To the extent that the American brand of constitutionalism binds us to the past, creates stability, and slows political change, how do we balance these conservative forces with the pressures of the moment that might demand departures from inherited ways of doing things and old ideas about rights and values? We sometimes change the terms of the old text through amendment or wholesale replacement of one constitution with another (from the Articles of Confederation to the Constitution at the national level, or more often at the state level), but we apply and adapt the inherited constitutional text through interpretation and practice. All the while, we manage the tension between being faithful to the text that we have and embracing the "living constitution" that grows out of that text.

Law figures prominently in the American constitutional tradition. Our written constitutions are understood to be fundamental laws and part of our legal code. They are the foundation of our legal system and superior to all other laws. They provide legally enforceable rules for judges and others to follow. Judges and lawyers play an important role in interpreting American constitutions and translating the bare bones of the original text into the detailed body of doctrine known as constitutional law. It has often been the dream of judges, lawyers, and legal scholars to insulate constitutional law from the world of politics. There is a long-held aspiration for judges and lawyers to be able to spin out constitutional law in accord with established principles of justice, reason, and tradition. But politics has also been central to the history of American constitutionalism. Constitutions are created by political actors and serve political purposes. Once in place, constitutional rules and values are politically contested, and they are interpreted and put into practice by politicians and political activists, as well as by judges. The tension between law and politics is a persistent one in American constitutional history.

A final tension of note has been between power and liberty. In the modern tradition, constitutional government is limited government. Constitutions impose limits and create mechanisms for making those constraints effective. They specify what the boundaries of government power are and what rights individuals and groups have against government. But there is also an older tradition, in which constitutions organize and empower government. The U.S. Constitution contains both elements. Many of its provisions, especially the amendments, limit government. These are some of the most celebrated features of the Constitution, and they have become the basis for much of the constitutional law that has been developed by the judiciary. But the Constitution was specifically adopted to empower the federal government and create new, better institutions that could accomplish national objectives. Both the U.S. Constitution and the state constitutions are designed to gather and direct government power to advance the public good. Throughout American constitutional history, judges, politicians, and activists have struggled over the proper balance between empowering government and limiting government and over the best understanding of the rights of individuals and the public welfare.

These essays examine American constitutionalism, not a particular constitutional text. The U.S. Constitution figures prominently in these essays, as it does in American history, but the American constitutional tradition includes other foundational documents, including notably the state constitutions. These texts are a guide to the subject matter of these essays, but they are not exhaustive of it. Laws, court decisions, administrative actions, and custom, along with founding documents, perform constitutional functions in the American political system, just as they do in the British system where there is no single written "constitution." Whether "written" or "unwritten," constitutions perform certain common tasks. Constitutions define the organic structures of government, specifying the basic institutions for making and implementing public policy, including the processes for altering the constitution itself. Constitutions distribute powers among those institutions of government, delegating, enumerating, prohibiting, and reserving powers to each governmental body. The flip side of entrusting power and discretion to governmental bodies is the definition of limits on those powers, the specification of individual and collective rights. Constitutions also specify who participates in the institutions of government and how and to whom the power of government applies. That is, constitutions identify the structures of citizenship and political jurisdiction. Across its seven articles and twenty-seven amendments, the U.S. Constitution addresses all of these topics, but the text is only a starting point. These topics form the subject matter of New Essays on American Constitutional History.

Writing early in the twentieth century, the great constitutional historian Edward Corwin observed that relatively few citizens actually read the U.S. Constitution, despite its brevity. He thought that this was in part because the "real constitution of the United States has come to mean something very different from the document" itself. The document laid out the framework of government, but "the real scope of the powers which it should exercise and of the rights which it should guarantee was left, to a very great extent, for future developments to determine." Understanding American constitutionalism requires understanding American constitutional history. It is a history of contestation and change, creation and elaboration. These essays aim to illuminate that history.

—*Keith E. Whittington,*
Princeton University

—*Gerry Leonard,*
Boston University School of Law

Introduction

he Constitution of 1787 did not mention the word "race." Indeed, someone unfamiliar with the history of the United States could read the document written in 1787 and never know that African Americans lived in the nation or that slavery was a central economic and social institution at the nation's founding. The only explicit reference to race or ethnicity in the document produced in Philadelphia concerns Indians, who are essentially treated as members of foreign nations.[1]

Despite the absence of the words slave or slavery, the Constitution contained a number of provisions that were directly related to slavery. Southern supporters of the Constitution praised it because it protected slavery in so many ways. Similarly, many opponents of the Constitution claimed it was a proslavery document, and many nineteenth-century abolitionists and modern scholars have agreed with this analysis. This view is further enhanced by a series of proslavery Supreme Court decisions, such as *Prigg v. Pennsylvania* (1842), *Jones v. Van Zandt* (1847), and *Dred Scott v. Sandford* (1857), which not only protected slavery, but shaped America's jurisprudence on race.

After the Civil War the United States adopted three new constitutional amendments—the thirteenth, fourteenth, and fifteenth—which were at a minimum designed to end slavery, make all people born in the nation citizens without regard to race, prohibit states from discriminating on the basis of race, and guarantee the right to vote without regard to race or previous status as slaves. Had the promise of these amendments been achieved, race discrimination, at least on a formal level, would have quickly disappeared. Many blacks might have remained disproportionately poor, but with access to schools, jobs, land, and political power, the history of African Americans in the United States would have been vastly different.

However, the courts by-and-large refused to use the new amendments to protect the rights of blacks, and after 1875 supporters of black rights in Congress never had enough political clout to pass protective legislation. Thus, by the end of the nineteenth century slavery no longer existed and blacks and Asians—who had begun to arrive in the United States in the late 1840s—had some basic rights, but substantial government-sanctioned discrimination at the state level was almost universally permitted.[2] Moreover, private discrimination was common, unrestrained by the Constitution, and often perfectly legal under state law. This meant that in most northern states racial minorities had formal equality, protected by state constitutional provisions and civil rights laws passed mostly in the last two decades of the century, as well as some substantive equality, and in some places protection against private discrimination, while in the South segregation was rampant. In the western states Asian immigrants and their American-born children often faced significant legal discrimination. In addition, federal laws and policies discriminated against Asian immigrants and prohibited them from becoming naturalized citizens.

1

Race and Slavery under the Constitution

he word "slavery" appears in only one place in the Constitution, in the Thirteenth Amendment, where the institution is abolished.[3] Some antebellum politicians and a few abolitionists, as well as some modern scholars, have argued that the refusal of the delegates to use the term slavery in the Constitution shows their embarrassment with the system, underscores their opposition to slavery, and indicates that they expected slavery to disappear soon. The records of debates at the Philadelphia Convention and the final text of the Constitution show the fundamental weakness of these arguments.

Throughout the convention debates the delegates frankly talked about "blacks," "Negroes," and "slaves." For example, on June 30, 1787, James Madison told the convention that "the States were divided into different interests not by their difference of size, but by other circumstances; the most material of which resulted partly from climate, but principally from (the effects of) their having or not having slaves." Two weeks later he made the same point: "It seemed now to be pretty well understood that the real difference of interests lay, not between the large & small but between the N. & Southn. States. The institution of slavery & its consequences formed the line of discrimination." Similarly, in discussing the direct election of the president, Hugh Williamson of North Carolina noted that if the president were elected by a popular vote, Virginia would suffer because "her slaves will have no suffrage." While James Madison believed "the people at large" were "the fittest" to choose the president, he rejected a popular election of the president because under such a scheme the southern states "could have no influence in the election on the score of the Negroes." In a heated debate over representation Gouverneur Morris, who represented Pennsylvania at the convention, declared that he could "never ... concur in upholding domestic slavery," which was "the curse of heaven on the States where it prevailed." He concluded that counting slaves for representation "when fairly explained comes to this: that the inhabitant of Georgia and S.C. who goes to the Coast of Africa, and in defiance of the most sacred laws of humanity tears away his fellow creatures from their dearest connections and dam[n]s them to the most cruel bondages, shall have more votes in a Govt. instituted for protection of the rights of mankind, than the Citizen of Pa. or N. Jersey who views with a laudable horror, so nefarious a practice." In the debate over the slave trade, Charles Pinckney of South Carolina declared that "slavery" was "justified by the example of all the world," and after noting slavery was found in "Greece Rome & other antient States," he boldly declared that "In all ages one half of mankind have been slaves." Similarly, Pierce Butler of South Carolina insisted that the Constitution protect slavery: "The security the Southn. States want is that their negroes may not be taken from them which some gentlemen within or without doors, have a very good mind to do."[4] Madison, Williamson, Morris, Pinckney, and Butler, like all the other delegates, were direct and blunt in their discussions of slavery.[5]

Despite the common use of the words "slave" and "Negro" in the debates, the final document avoided these terms, using euphemisms instead. The language in the final document was clearly designed to make the Constitution more palatable to the North. In a debate over representation, William Paterson of New Jersey claimed that the Congress under the Articles of Confederation "had been ashamed to use the term 'Slaves' & had substituted a description."[6] This issue came up at the convention again during the debate over the African slave trade. The delegates from the Carolinas and Georgia vigorously demanded that the African trade remain open under the new Constitution. Gouverneur Morris of Pennsylvania, unable to contain his anger over this immoral compromise, suggested that the proposed clause read: the "Importation of slaves into N. Carolina, S-- Carolina & Georgia" shall not be prohibited. Connecticut's Roger Sherman, who voted with the Deep South to allow the trade, objected, not only to the singling out of specific states, but also to the term slave. He declared he "liked a description better than the terms proposed, which had been declined by the old Congs & were not pleasing to some people." George Clymer of Pennsylvania "concurred with Mr. Sherman" on this issue.[7] In the North Carolina ratifying convention James Iredell, who had been a delegate in Philadelphia, explained that "the word slave is not mentioned" because "[t]he northern delegates, owing to their particular scruples on the subject of slavery, did not choose the word slave to be mentioned."[8] Thus, southerners avoided the term because they did not want unnecessarily to antagonize their colleagues from the North. As long as they were assured of protection for their institution, the southerners at the convention were willing to do without the word "slave." A majority of the northern delegates meanwhile avoided the term, not because they were ashamed of the many proslavery provisions in the Constitution, but because they feared their own constituents might object to such terminology.

Despite the circumlocution, the Constitution directly sanctioned slavery in five provisions:

Art. I, § 2. Cl. 3. The three-fifths clause provided for counting three-fifths of all slaves for purposes of allocating representation in Congress among the states. This clause also provided that, if any "direct tax" was levied on the states, it could be imposed only proportionately, according to population, and that only three-fifths of all slaves would be counted in assessing what each state's contribution would be. (However, almost no one at the Convention imagined there would ever be direct taxes.[9])

Art. I, § 9, Cl. 1. This clause prohibited Congress from banning the "Migration or Importation of such Persons as any of the States now existing shall think proper to admit" before the year 1808. Awkwardly phrased and seemingly purposefully designed to confuse readers, this clause prevented Congress from ending the African slave trade before 1808, but did not require Congress to ban the trade after that date. The clause was a significant exception to the general power granted to Congress to regulate all international commerce.

Art. I, § 9, Cl. 4. This clause declared that any "capitation" or other "direct tax" had to take into account the three-fifths clause. It ensured that, if a head tax were ever levied, slaves would be taxed at three-fifths the rate of free people.

Art. IV, § 2, Cl. 3. The fugitive slave clause prohibited the states from emancipating fugitive slaves and required that runaways be returned to their owners "on demand."

Art. V. This article prohibited any amendment of the slave importation or capitation clauses before 1808.

Taken together, these five provisions gave the South a strong claim to "special treatment" for its peculiar institution. The three-fifths clause also gave the South extra political muscle—in the House of Representatives and in the Electoral College—to support that claim.

Numerous other clauses of the Constitution supplemented the five clauses that directly protected slavery. Some provisions that indirectly guarded slavery, such as the prohibition on taxing exports, were included primarily to protect the interests of slaveholders and the slave states. Others, such as the guarantee of federal support to "suppress Insurrections" and the creation of the Electoral College, were written with slavery in mind, although delegates also supported them for reasons having nothing to do with slavery. The most prominent indirect protections of slavery were:

Art. I, § 8, Cl. 15. The domestic insurrections clause empowered Congress to call "forth the Militia" to "suppress Insurrections," including slave rebellions. Although the Framers certainly had more than slave insurrections in mind, the abolitionist Wendell Phillips considered this to be one of the most important proslavery clauses because it gave slaveholders protection from their slaves. Southern supporters of the Constitution agreed, while some northern anti-federalists opposed the Constitution because as members of their state militias they did not want to have to protect the southern master class from its slaves.

Art. I, § 9, Cl. 5. This clause prohibited federal taxes on exports and thus prevented an indirect tax on slavery by taxing the staple products of slave labor, such as tobacco, rice, and eventually cotton. Like the slave trade provision, the ban on export taxes was a significant limitation on the power of Congress to regulate international commerce through export duties. These two provisions—both designed to protect slavery—were the only substantive limitations on Congress's power to regulate international commerce in the Constitution.

Art. I, § 10, Cl. 2. This clause prohibited the *states* from taxing exports or imports, thus preventing an indirect tax on the products of slave labor by a nonslaveholding state. This was especially important to the slave states because almost all products of the slave states—tobacco, rice, and eventually cotton—were shipped out of northern ports.

Art. II, § 1, Cl. 2. This clause provided for the indirect election of the president through an Electoral College based on congressional representation. This provision incorporated the three-fifths clause into the Electoral College and gave whites in slave states a disproportionate influence in the election of the president. This clause had a major impact on the politics of slavery as well as American history in general. Thomas Jefferson's victory in the election of 1800 would be possible only because of the electoral votes the southern states gained on account of their slaves. Thus Jefferson, who spent most of his career either avoiding any conflict over slavery or protecting slavery, was elevated to the presidency in part because of slavery.[10]

Art. IV, § 3, Cl. 1. This clause allowed for the admission of new states. The delegates to the Convention anticipated the admission of new slave states to the Union.

Art. IV, § 4. In this provision, known as the guarantee clause, the United States government promised to protect states from "domestic Violence," including slave rebellions.

Art. V. By requiring a three-fourths majority of the states to ratify any amendment to the Constitution, this article ensured that the slaveholding states would have a perpetual veto over any constitutional changes. The importance of this clause is more apparent if we imagine there had been no Civil War and thus no emancipation. Had all fifteen slave states remained in the Union, they would to this day be able to prevent an amendment on any subject. In a fifty-state union, it takes only thirteen states to block any amendment.

Finally, some clauses did not inherently favor slavery, and were not necessarily considered to affect slavery when they were debated, but ultimately protected the institution when interpreted by the courts or implemented by Congress. It would be wrong to argue that these illustrate the proslavery nature of the Constitutional Convention. However, these clauses do illustrate how the proslavery tone of the Constitution and the many explicit protections of slavery encouraged Congress, the executive branch, and the courts—if they needed any such encouragement—to interpret seemingly neutral clauses in favor of slavery. Such clauses also directly challenge historian William W. Freehling's argument that the Framers were inherently antislavery and that "[t]he impact of the Founding Fathers on slavery ... must be seen in the long run not in terms of what changed in the late eighteenth century but in terms of how the Revolutionary experience changed the whole of American antebellum history."[11] If we look at the "long run" impact of the Constitution on "American antebellum history" we see that from 1820 until the Civil War Congress and the Supreme Court increasingly protected slavery. Rather than weakening slavery, the proslavery clauses in the Constitution strengthened it.

The application of the following clauses, which were used to protect slavery, not to harm it, show the general proslavery tenor of the Constitution and the government created under it. Some of these clauses also helped create a race-based jurisprudence that led to discrimination against nonwhites more generally.

Art. I, § 8, Cl. 4. The naturalization clause gave Congress exclusive power to regulate naturalization of aliens. Before the Civil War, Congress used this power to prohibit the naturalization of nonwhites and after 1875 continued to prohibit Asian immigrants from becoming citizens. Congress changed this in the mid-twentieth century. Had naturalization remained in the hands of the states, as it had been under the Articles of Confederation, it is likely that some of the states, especially those which granted substantial equality, or even just some equality, to blacks, would have also allowed foreign-born nonwhites to become citizens.

Art. I, § 8, Cl. 17. The clause that provided for the District of Columbia allowed Congress to regulate institutions, including slavery, in what became the national capital. Under this clause Congress allowed slavery in Washington, D.C., and protected the institution in a variety of ways.

Art. III, § 2, Cl. 1. The diversity jurisdiction clause limited the right to sue in federal courts to "Citizens of different States," rather than inhabitants. In *Dred Scott v. Sandford* the Supreme Court would interpret this clause to prohibit blacks from suing in federal court.

Art. IV, § 1. The full faith and credit clause required each state to grant legal recognition to the laws and judicial proceedings of other states, thus obligating free states to recognize laws creating and protecting slavery.

Art. IV, § 2, Cl. 1. The privileges and immunities clause required that states grant equal privileges and immunities to "citizens" of other states. In the antebellum period southern whites were given privileges and immunities when visiting the North, but the southern states not only refused to give such rights to free blacks from the North, but often arrested them if they even entered their jurisdictions. Congress or the courts might have acted to protect the right of northern black citizens to travel everywhere in the United States. However, Congress refused to consider legislation to protect the privileges and immunities of free blacks. The courts dodged the issue until *Dred Scott* when the Supreme Court held that the Constitution provided no protection for free blacks, even those who could vote and hold office in the states where they lived.

Art. IV, § 3, Cl. 2. This clause allowed Congress the power to regulate the territories. In 1820 Congress used this clause to limit slavery in the territories, but in *Dred Scott v. Sandford* the Supreme Court ruled that the clause authorized Congress to protect slavery in the territories, but not to ban the institution.

In addition to the specific clauses of the Constitution that protected slavery, the entire structure of the document protected slaveholders against emancipation of their slaves by the new federal government. Because the Constitution created a government of limited powers, Congress lacked the power to interfere in the domestic institutions of the states. Thus, during the ratification debates, only the most fearful southern anti-federalists opposed the Constitution on the grounds that it threatened slavery. Most southerners, even those who opposed the Constitution for other reasons, agreed with General Charles Cotesworth Pinckney of South Carolina, who crowed to his state's house of representatives:

> We have a security that the general government can never emancipate them, for no such authority is granted and it is admitted, on all hands, that the general government has no powers but what are expressly granted by the Constitution, and that all rights not expressed were reserved by the several states.[12]

The Constitution was not "essentially open-ended with respect to slavery," as historian Don Fehrenbacher argued.[13] On the contrary, the Constitution provided enormous protections for the peculiar institution of the South at very little cost to that region. At the Virginia ratifying convention, Edmund Randolph denied that the Constitution posed any threat at all to slavery. He challenged opponents of the Constitution, "Where is the part that has a tendency to the abolition of slavery?" He answered his own question: "Were it right here to mention what passed in [the Philadelphia] convention ... I might tell you that the Southern States, even South Carolina herself, conceived this property to be secure" and that "there was not a member of the Virginia delegation who had the smallest suspicion of the abolition of slavery." South Carolinians would have agreed with Randolph. In summing up the entire Constitution, General Charles Cotesworth Pinckney, who had been one of the ablest defenders of slavery at the Convention, proudly told the South Carolina House of Representatives: "In short, considering all circumstances, we have made the best terms for the security of this species of property it was in our power to make. We would have made better if we could; but on the whole, I do not think them bad."[14] Pinckney had good reason to be proud of his role in Philadelphia. Throughout the Convention, he and other delegates from the Deep South tenaciously fought to protect the interests of slaveholders. In these struggles they were usually successful.

2

Implementing the Constitution: Slavery, Congress, and the Courts

etween 1789 and 1861 Congress passed numerous laws that affected slavery. Most, but not all, protected slavery and had a negative impact on the status of free blacks. All of these laws were part of implementing the new Constitution and putting flesh on the bones of the structure created in Philadelphia in 1787. Most of this statutory regulation eventually reached the Supreme Court. Invariably, the Court supported the interests of slave owners and slavery, at the expense of fugitive slaves, free blacks, and their white allies.

The African Slave Trade

Article I, Section 9 of the Constitution prohibited Congress from ending the African slave trade before January 1, 1808. Without the clause, the First Congress would have probably banned the slave trade. Most Americans viewed the trade with horror. Sentiment against it was strong in the Upper South, in part because of its inherent immorality, but also because Virginia and Maryland annually shipped thousands of slaves to South Carolina and Georgia, and a ban on the African trade would raise the value of these slaves. At the Constitutional Convention the South Carolina and Georgia delegations insisted on this clause to protect their right to import more slaves. The clause did not *require* an end to the slave trade, as many scholars have mistakenly argued. In fact, it made the indefinite perpetuation of the slave trade a real possibility. At the Constitutional Convention most delegates assumed the South would grow faster than the North. They also assumed that the states of the old Northwest, such as Ohio, would be sympathetic to slavery. If the southerners had been correct in these assumptions, then by 1808 the Deep South, which supported a continuation of the African trade, might very well have been able to put together a coalition to block any law banning the trade. During the debates over ratification supporters of the Constitution in the North, as well as in Virginia and Maryland, came under intense pressure because of this clause. As one New York opponent put it, by supporting the Constitution, with its slave trade provision, he would be condoning "drenching the bowels of Africa in gore, for the sake of enslaving its free-born innocent inhabitants." Similarly an anti-federalist in Virginia ironically suggested that the slave trade provision was an "excellent clause" for "an Algerian constitution: but not so well calculated (I hope) for the latitude of America."[15] In an effort to defuse this opposition, supporters of the Constitution argued that the clause actually required an end to the trade in 1808. Some supporters of the Constitution also argued that the clause allowed Congress to end slavery in 1808. In the Pennsylvania ratifying convention James Wilson asserted that after "the lapse of a few years ... Congress will have power to exterminate slavery from within our borders."[16] Such arguments, however wrong or disingenuous they were, helped persuade some northerners to accept the Constitution. By the time the Constitution was ratified most Americans assumed that in 1808 the trade would come to an end. Meanwhile, Congress passed laws in 1794, 1800, and 1803 to completely ban any American participation in the trade. New slaves could still be brought into the country on foreign ships—more than 50,000 would come in between 1800 and 1808—but American citizens and American ships could not participate in the trade.

The statutes barring American participation in the trade, as well as assurances of supporters of ratification in the North and Upper South that the trade would end in 1808, led to a common perception with much of the general public that the trade *had to end* in 1808. This common understanding of the meaning of the slave trade clause—at least in the North and much of the Upper South—is probably the first example of "popular constitution-alism" in the new nation. Had the politics of the age been different—and the Deep South been politically more powerful than it was—the outcome might have been different. Instead, Virginians (who in part opposed the trade because it lowered the value of the slaves they were selling to the South) teamed up with northerners to hem in the trade as much as possible, with acts passed in 1794, 1800, and 1803. In his annual message to Congress in 1806 President Thomas Jefferson took a moment to "congratulate" his "fellow-citizens, on the approach of the period at which you may interpose your authority constitutionally to withdraw the citizens of the United States from all further participation in those violations of human rights which have been so long continued on the unoffending inhabitants of Africa, and which the morality, the reputation, and the best interests of our country have long been eager to proscribe." He noted that any law passed by Congress could not take effect until January 1, 1808, but he urged Congress to act quickly "to prevent by timely notice expeditions which can not be completed before that day." In March 1807 Congress readily complied, passing legislation to absolutely ban all importations of slaves after January 1, 1808. The 1807 act was a comprehensive attempt to close the African trade. By passing the law in March, Congress gave all international slave traders nine months to close down their operations going into the United States.[17]

Still, while legal imports stopped in 1808, the new law proved difficult to enforce. Americans continued to participate in the trade, bringing slaves both to the United States and to other countries. Initially, as discussed just below, the Marshall Court failed to uphold prosecutions under the law and overturned a number of convictions for slave trading for very narrow or technical reasons. This led to supplemental laws in 1818, 1819, and 1820, which provided support for enforcement. The last act made slave trading piracy, punishable by hanging, but the Marshall Court continued to limit the scope of slave-trading prosecutions.

The Supreme Court heard a number of cases dealing with the illegal trade. Before 1818 the Court tended to be skeptical of prosecutions of alleged traders, which were often brought before the ships actually went to sea, thus creating problems of proof as to whether the ship was actually being fitted for a slave trading voyage. Other prosecutions failed because they were brought only after the ships had returned from years-long African voyages. Since the offense began when the ship left an American port, it might return after the statute of limitations had expired. In *Adams v. Woods* (1805) Chief Justice Marshall rigidly applied the statute of limitations in just this way to protect a slave trader. Marshall simply turned a deaf ear to the obvious result of his analysis, that "[n]o vessel engaged in the slave trade" would "ever be subjected to condemnation; for the voyage is always circuitous, and generally takes up more than two years to perform it."[18] Similarly, in *Brig Caroline v. United States* (1813) the Court used questionable, technical arguments to prevent the prosecution of a trader. However, by the mid-1820s the Court was more supportive of prosecutions, and in *The Emily and the Caroline* (1824) the Court upheld convictions for ships that were seized before they left port.

While Congress had used its power to declare slave trading piracy, the Court refused to apply the law to all ships and ship captains. Thus, in a series of cases surrounding the ship *The Antelope* (1825 and 1827) the Court ordered some Africans freed because they were the fruit of the illegal trade, but allowed others to be sold because they were taken from Africa legally by a Spanish ship. *The Antelope* was a Spanish vessel captured on the high seas by pirates. On June 29, 1820, an American revenue cutter seized the *Antelope*, arrested her American captain under the 1807 and 1819 laws banning the slave trade, and towed the ship and its 258 African slaves to Savannah. Before its capture the *Antelope* had seized other ships involved in the trade; many of the blacks on board had initially been brought out of Africa on ships owned by citizens of various countries including Spain, Portugal, and the United States. After sorting out numerous claims, the trial court ordered that some of the slaves on the *Antelope* be returned to the Spanish government because these slaves were lawfully owned by Spanish subjects at the time the ship was captured in American waters. The remaining Africans, those claimed by Americans and others, were turned over to the U.S. government as the fruit of the illegal trade. Speaking for the Supreme Court, Chief Justice Marshall upheld this result.

Marshall noted that in this case the "sacred rights of liberty and property come in conflict with each other." In the end the Court, which had five southerners on it (Marshall, Bushrod Washington, William Johnson, Gabriel Duvall, and Thomas Todd) firmly supported the sacredness of property over liberty. Marshall admitted that the African slave trade was "contrary to the law of nature" but concluded that it was "consistent with the law of nations" and "cannot in itself be piracy."[19] Thus, the Court recognized the right of foreign nations to engage in the slave trade. Marshall wrote, "If it be neither repugnant to the law of nations, nor piracy, it is almost superfluous to say in this Court, that the right of bringing in for adjudication in time of peace, even where the vessel belongs to a nation which has prohibited the trade, cannot exist."[20] This analysis allowed the Court to uphold prosecutions against American traders because they violated the U.S. prohibition on the African trade, while also protecting the property rights in enslaved Africans owned by citizens of nations where the trade was legal. Because the *Antelope* had been found in American waters, the Court might have held that all the Africans were free because they had been brought into the United States, in violation of the federal ban on the African trade. However, it chose not to reach this result, thus favoring property over liberty and foreign law over domestic law.

The Court's most famous slave trade case, *The Amistad* (1841), involved Africans brought to Cuba in violation of Cuban law. The case turned on the status of these Africans and on the interpretation of a 1795 treaty with Spain. Justice Joseph Story acknowledged that if the blacks on the *Amistad* were Cuban and legally enslaved there, they would "justly be deemed within the intent of the treaty" and be returned to Cuba. But Story found "it is beyond controversy, if we examine the evidence, that these negroes never were the lawful slaves" under Cuban law. It was manifestly clear that they were "natives of Africa, and were kidnapped there, and were unlawfully transported to Cuba, in violation of the laws and treaties of Spain, and the most solemn edicts and declarations of that government." Story concluded that "these negroes are not slaves" but had been "kidnapped" and were "entitled to their freedom."[21]

The *Amistad* case was famous at the time, and used by abolitionists to teach Americans about the evils of slavery. Abolitionists used the case to raise money for their cause, expose the ongoing illegal trade to Cuba, and demonstrate how the Van Buren administration favored slavery over freedom. The plight of the "Amistads," as the Africans on the ship were called, humanized slavery and helped drive home the point that all American slaves were the descendants of people like the Amistads—free people living in Africa who were kidnapped and brought to the New World in chains. The logic of the case was that if it was wrong to enslave native-born Africans in the 1840s then it must be wrong to keep in slavery the descendants of those kidnapped at an earlier time. But, while the case provided an excellent educational opportunity for the antislavery movement, the decision itself was not antislavery per se, because the outcome turned entirely on the text of a treaty with Spain and the fact that the Amistads had been brought to Cuba in violation of Spanish law. Indeed, while the Court held that the Amistads were free, it also held that a Cuban-born slave on the ship who had been a cabin boy had to be returned to Cuba. Jurisprudentially, the case had no subsequent impact on the development of American law.

Although federal law provided for the execution of captains participating in the illegal African trade, no one was executed under the law until the Lincoln administration came into office. In *Ex parte Gordon* (1862) the Supreme Court upheld a death penalty conviction under the 1820 ban on the slave trade. In 1865 the Court upheld prosecutions against four ships that were being equipped to participate in the illegal slave trade with Cuba.

The slave trade provision was a limitation on congressional power. Had the clause not been in the Constitution, the first Congress would most likely have banned the trade. Because of the clause forbidding Congress from ending the trade, more than 50,000 Africans were brought to the United States, mostly between 1803 and 1808. Ultimately the Court joined the legislative and executive branches in stopping the trade. While preventing the importation of new slaves to the United States, the ban on the trade had no effect on the legal status of bondage within the nation.

Fugitive Slaves

Article IV of the Constitution set out general rules for the return of fugitives from justice:

> A Person charged in any State with Treason, Felony, or other Crime, who shall flee from Justice, and be found in another State, shall on Demand of the executive Authority of the State from which he fled, be delivered up, to be removed to the State having Jurisdiction of the Crime.

The same article also provided for the return of fugitive slaves, although the process, as set out in the clause, was not clear:

> No Person held to Service or Labour in one State, under the Laws thereof, escaping into another, shall, in Consequence of any Law or Regulation therein, be discharged from such Service or Labour, but shall be delivered up on Claim of the Party to whom such Service or Labour may be due.

Unlike the clause regulating fugitives from justice, which contemplated an interaction between governors, the fugitive slave clause gave no hint of how it was to be enforced. The text of the clause assumed that fugitive slaves would be easily recognized and that when found in another state they would be held by someone who could "deliver" them "up" when claimed by a master or the agent of a master. Thus the clause implicitly was about race. While a few white indentured servants or apprentices might be recovered under the clause, the focus of the provision was fugitive slaves, who would be identified by their race.

Because both clauses were found in Article IV, which primarily dealt with interstate relations, it would have been plausible for Congress to have concluded that it had no power to implement these provisions. However, in 1793 Congress passed the nation's first extradition statute that set out procedures for the return of both fugitive slaves and fugitives from justice. The law empowered all state and federal judges in the country to issue certificates of removal to allow a master to take a fugitive slave back to the state from which he or she escaped. The certificate was to be issued "upon proof to the satisfaction of such Judge or magistrate, either by oral testimony or affidavit taken before and certified by a magistrate of any such State or Territory" that the person seized was a fugitive slave.[22] This standard left much to judicial discretion and was likely to lead to free blacks being seized as fugitives.

The Supreme Court did not hear a case under this law until *Prigg v. Pennsylvania* (1842). Speaking for an 8–1 majority, Justice Joseph Story upheld the constitutionality of the 1793 law with an opinion that threatened the liberty of all free blacks in the North, as the factual background of *Prigg* itself illustrated. The case stemmed from the refusal of a Pennsylvania justice of the peace to give Prigg and three other men a certificate of removal to take Jerry and Margaret Morgan and their children to Maryland as fugitive slaves. At least one of Morgan's children had been born in Pennsylvania, and was thus free under that state's law. Margaret Morgan had never before been claimed as a slave by anyone. Her parents had been slaves whose master allowed them to live as free people. In 1830, while she still lived in Maryland, the U.S. Census recorded Margaret as a free woman, married to Jerry Morgan, who had been born free in Pennsylvania. When the justice of the peace refused to grant the certificate, Prigg and three other men seized Margaret and her children—but not her Pennsylvania-born husband—and forcibly took them to Maryland. Prigg was later convicted of kidnapping and appealed this conviction to the Supreme Court.[23]

Justice Story ignored the fact the Margaret Morgan had lived her life entirely as a free woman and that at least one of her children had been born in Pennsylvania, and was thus a free person from birth. He ruled that the states could not interfere in the return of fugitive slaves or add extra demands for proof beyond those set out in the federal law. This meant that free blacks like at least one of Morgan's children—and perhaps Morgan herself—could be dragged to the South as slaves.[24] Even more significantly, Story asserted that a master did not actually have to comply with the 1793 law to remove a fugitive slave. Story asserted that the constitutional clause gave masters a common law right to recapture their slaves wherever they were found, as long as the capture could be done without a breach of the peace. This was an open invitation for kidnappers to seize any blacks in the North they might find, fugitive or free, and bring them South under the claim they had done so by asserting their common law right of recaption. Justice John McLean, who was from Ohio, bitterly dissented from this result, complaining that it would lead to kidnapping. But he was a lone voice on a Court determined to protect slavery and utterly uninterested in the fate of African Americans, even those who were free. In this case Justice Story nationalized the law of slavery and the South, allowing masters to seize blacks anywhere they found them, and bring them back to a southern state for a determination on their status as slaves or free people. For Story and all of the other justices except John McLean, placating the South was more important than upholding the law of freedom in the North or respecting the liberty of free blacks. *Prigg* was thus a precursor to *Dred Scott*, as Story found that free blacks in the North had no rights if seized as fugitive slaves and the free states had no legal power to protect the liberty of their free black citizens.

The only positive aspect of this opinion, from the perspective of blacks and their white allies, was Story's conclusion that while state officials could not interfere with the return of a fugitive slave, they could also not be compelled to hear such cases. At the time there were very few federal judges and federal marshals—only one or two in a state—and without judges to hear cases and police officials to aid in the return of fugitive slaves, masters might find it difficult to recover their runaway slaves. The right of recaption—such as Prigg exercised against Margaret Morgan—might work along the border between slavery and freedom, such as southeastern Pennsylvania or southern Ohio, Indiana, and Illinois, but it would be more difficult to implement further north. Justice Taney in a separate opinion attacked this part of Story's opinion, complaining that state officials should be required to enforce the law. Story himself understood the problem and privately wrote to Senator John M. Berrien of Georgia, urging him to sponsor a bill to create commissioners throughout the nation to hear any case under federal law that a state judge could hear. Story argued this could be done without even mentioning the fugitive slave issue, but would result in national enforcement of the 1793 law.

In *Jones v. Van Zandt* (1847) the Court further imperiled free blacks by holding a white man financially liable for the escape of slaves he met walking on a road in Ohio. John Van Zandt gave a ride in his wagon to a group of blacks walking along a road in southern Ohio. He claimed he had no way of knowing they were slaves, that he had no legal notice that they were claimed as slaves, and that in Ohio all people were presumed free. Justice John McLean heard this case while riding circuit. McLean was the only member of the Court openly hostile to slavery, but he nevertheless accepted his obligation to enforce the fugitive slave law. Van Zandt was a well-known abolitionist and the jury, under McLean's direction, believed that he had in fact knowingly aided these fugitive slaves.[25] The U.S. Supreme Court agreed with McLean's circuit opinion and rejected Van Zandt's argument that he had a right to offer a ride to anyone in Ohio, unless he had legal notice the person was a slave. The Court concluded that he should have assumed the blacks walking along the road were fugitives and by giving them a ride he could be sued for the cost of recapturing them and for the value of one who was never recaptured. While the facts might have supported the outcome, Justice Levi Woodbury's opinion undermined black freedom in the North by putting whites on notice that if they helped blacks, who turned out to be fugitive slaves, they could be sued for enormous damages. Van Zandt died before his case was finally over, but almost all of his assets were eventually lost to the slaveowner, Wharton Jones.

In the Compromise of 1850 Congress banned the public sale of slaves in the District of Columbia, which was a symbolic blow at slavery that had no practical effect on bondage in the national capital. At most it forced masters to cross the Potomac River into Alexandria to engage in the domestic trade. The compromise also brought California into the Union as a free state, thus giving the nonslave states a majority in the Senate. The cost of these concessions was high. The compromise allowed slavery in all of the territories acquired in the Mexican War (except California), which was a partial repeal of the Missouri Compromise line, and held the promise of new slaves states in the West. Most importantly, Congress passed a new and controversial fugitive slave law, which created a national enforcement mechanism, with the appointment of federal commissioners in every county. This law was very similar to the proposal outlined by Justice Story in his letter to Senator Berrien after *Prigg*. This was the first time in U.S. history that the federal government established a law enforcement presence throughout the nation. The new law provided summary proceedings for fugitive slaves, allowed judges and U.S. marshals to call out the militia or call on the military to return runaways, prohibited states from interfering in any way with the return of fugitive slaves, and explicitly denied alleged fugitives the right to testify at their own hearing or to have a jury determine their status. Thus, race led to a legal presumption that would prevent a free person from testifying on his own behalf that he was being mistaken for a fugitive slave. The law provided severe jail sentences and heavy fines for anyone interfering with the return of a fugitive. From the moment he signed the law, President Millard Filmore and his successors vigorously enforced it. The Court upheld this law in *Ableman v. Booth* (1859).

The fugitive slave laws and the Court's implementation of them jeopardized the liberty of all blacks in the free states while placing the U.S. government firmly on the side of slaveholders' rights. Had it not been for *Dred Scott v. Sandford* (1857), which is discussed below, the *Prigg* case would be remembered as the most proslavery decision the Court ever rendered. Most importantly, the fugitive slave clause, the laws implementing it, and the cases enforcing it underscored the nation's commitment to slavery and the constitutional regime that used race as a basis for determining legal rights and legal status.

Slavery in the Territories and Black Citizenship

Even before the Constitution was written the national government faced the problem of slavery spreading to the western territories. In July 1787 the Congress under the Articles of Confederation passed the Northwest Ordinance, which prohibited slavery north and west of the Ohio River. After ratification of the Constitution, the new Congress reenacted the ordinance. The ordinance did not immediately free any slaves and as late as the 1840s a small number of blacks were held in bondage in Illinois. Moreover, the ordinance did not require that free blacks be granted any equality. Eventually six free states—Ohio, Indiana, Illinois, Michigan, Wisconsin, and part of Minnesota—would be carved out of this region, but none of them granted blacks full equality, although by 1860 only Illinois and Indiana restricted black in-migration or prohibited them from testifying against whites. Furthermore, neither the Articles of Confederation Congress nor the national Congress under the Constitution prohibited slavery in the Southwest, thus setting the stage for the admission of Kentucky, Tennessee, Mississippi, and Alabama as slave states.

In 1803 the nation acquired vast lands west of the Mississippi as part of the Louisiana Purchase. Congress did not initially regulate slavery in the area, and in 1812 admitted Louisiana as a slave state. In 1819 Missouri too sought admission as a slave state, but this led to a two-year debate over slavery in the new state. Northerners tried to bring Missouri into the Union as a free state and require it to allow free blacks to enter the state. In the end the Compromise of 1820—also known as the Missouri Compromise— brought Missouri into the Union as a slave state, but banned slavery north and west of the southern boundary of that state. The Missouri Compromise was a political arrangement that achieved almost constitutional status in the minds of many Americans, especially in the North. Many northerners considered the compromise almost sacred, representing a commitment, along with the Northwest Ordinance, to eventually end slavery. Events, however, moved in the opposite direction. Subsequent acquisitions of Florida, Texas, and the Mexican Cession led to slavery spreading across new territories and states. Then, in 1850 and 1854, Congress opened most of the remaining western territories to slavery, including those formerly governed by the Missouri Compromise.

In *Dred Scott v. Sandford* (1857) the Supreme Court pushed this trend a step further, holding that Congress had no power to ban slavery in the territories. Dred Scott, a Missouri slave, sued for his freedom because he had lived in what is today Minnesota, where slavery was banned under the Missouri Compromise. Scott's owner at the time of the suit was John Sanford, who lived in New York.[26] The Constitution allows a citizen of one state to sue a citizen of another state in federal court. Scott claimed that as a free man he was a citizen of Missouri, and thus able to sue Sanford in federal court.

Writing for a 7–2 majority, Chief Justice Roger B. Taney rejected Scott's claim of freedom on a variety of grounds. First, he ruled that free blacks could never be citizens of the United States and thus Dred Scott had no standing to sue in federal court, even if he was legally entitled to be free. This should have ended the case because the Court, under Taney's theory, had no jurisdiction over the case. Critics of the decision, such as Abraham Lincoln, would later argue that everything Taney said about the territories was merely *dicta*, and had no legal force because once Taney ruled that Scott could not bring a suit as a citizen of Missouri, the case was over.

However, a majority of the Court supported Taney's long proslavery analysis of congressional power over slavery and the territories. Whether *dicta* or not, the Court held on two separate grounds that Congress could not ban slavery in the territories, and that the ban on slavery in the Missouri Compromise was unconstitutional. First, Taney held that slaves constituted a constitutionally protected form of private property, such that it would violate the Fifth Amendment to "deprive" slaveowners of their "property" just because they brought it into territories owned collectively by all the people of the United States. Here Taney concluded Congress had no power to prohibit citizens from taking their legally held slave property into federal territories that were owned by all Americans. He asserted "an act of Congress which deprives a citizen of the United States of his liberty or property, merely because he came himself or brought his property into a particular Territory of the United States, and who had committed no offence against the laws, could hardly be dignified with the name of due process of law."[27]

In reaching this conclusion, Chief Justice Taney held that Congress had no power to pass any laws limiting the right to own slaves in the territories and, furthermore, that while territorial legislatures were the proper bodies to pass laws for the territories they could not ban slavery either. Just as Justice Story had nationalized the law of slavery for fugitive slaves in his *Prigg* decision, Chief Justice Taney nationalized it for the territories. Freedom was now, under federal law, a local option, that ran counter to the national rule, which was to favor slavery. This holding shocked many northerners, who argued that since 1787 Congress had been regulating slavery in the territories, and as recently as the Kansas-Nebraska Act of 1854, had claimed the power to ban slavery in the territories or allow the settlers to do so.

Taney also held that, except for launching a basic governing structure, Congress had no right to pass laws for the territories. The U.S. Constitution provided that "Congress shall have Power to dispose of and make all needful Rules and Regulations respecting the Territory or other Property belonging to the United States."[28] But Taney, with the support of the majority of the Court, held that this provision only applied to the territories that existed in 1787 and did not apply to the territories west of the Mississippi, acquired after the Constitution went into effect. Since 1789 Congress had passed all sorts of legislation regulating the territories. Northerners were now being told scores of statutes dealing with slavery in the territories, as well as laws regulating other aspects of the territories, were all unconstitutional. The northern reaction to this portion of the decision helped make the Republican Party the dominant political organization in the North and led to Lincoln's election to the presidency in 1860.

Equally shocking, Chief Justice Taney asserted that even if Dred Scott were free he could not sue in federal court, because no black could ever be a citizen of the United States.[29] The way Taney framed the issue in his opinion indicates his determination to decide the status of blacks in America generally, not just the status of Dred Scott. Taney wrote,

> The question is simply this: Can a negro, whose ancestors were imported into this country, and sold as slaves, become a member of the political community formed and brought into existence by the Constitution of the United States, and as such become entitled to all the rights, and privileges, and immunities, guaranteed by that instrument to the citizen? One of which rights is the privilege of suing in a court of the United States in the cases specified in the Constitution.[30]

Taney argued that free blacks—even those who were allowed to vote and hold public office in the states where they lived—could never be citizens of the United States and have standing to sue in federal courts. Here Taney asserted —invented really—a concept of dual citizenship. He argued that being a citizen of a state did not necessarily make one a citizen of the United States.

Taney's argument is at odds with the text of the Constitution itself, which never defined a citizen of the United States, but only referred to citizens of the "states." Indeed, throughout the Constitution notions of national citizenship are tied to state citizenship. The right to vote for national legislators, for example, which is found in Article I, Sec. 2 of the Constitution, was tied to the right to vote for members of the state legislature. Thus, oddly, under Taney's theory free blacks in a number of states could vote for members of the state legislature, members of Congress, and in presidential elections, but were somehow *not* citizens of the United States. Article III, Sec. 2 provides for a right to sue in federal courts when "Citizens of different States" sued each other. Article IV, Sec. 1 requires the states to grant citizens of other states equal "Privileges and Immunities," which implies that citizenship in one state gives you certain rights as a citizen throughout the country. Thus, before *Dred Scott* most Americans assumed that anyone who was considered a citizen of a state was also a citizen of the United States. Even Taney had recognized this, asserting in the *Passenger Cases* that "every citizen of a State is also a citizen of the United States."[31] In that case he had argued that the Constitution gave Congress the power to regulate naturalization, to prevent the states from naturalizing people who the other states found unacceptable as citizens. He argued that the "sole object" of the naturalization clause "was to prevent one State from forcing upon all the others, and upon the general government, persons as citizens whom they were unwilling to admit as such."[32] Taney now extended this principle to what he deemed as unacceptable people. Thus, blacks could not be citizens of the United States, even if they had birthright state citizenship. In claiming that blacks could never be citizens of the United States, Taney backed away from the idea that all state citizens were also national citizens. He now argued,

> In discussing this question, we must not confound the rights of citizenship which a State may confer within its own limits, and the rights of citizenship as a member of the Union. It does not by any means follow, because he has all the rights and privileges of a citizen of a State, that he must be a citizen of the United States. He may have all of the rights and privileges of the citizen of a State, and yet not be entitled to the rights and privileges of a citizen in any other State.[33]

Taney based this novel argument entirely on race. He offered a slanted and one-sided history of the founding period which ignored the fact that free blacks had voted in a number of states at the time of the ratification of the Constitution. Despite this history (which Justices McLean and Curtis set out in their dissents), the Chief Justice insisted that at the Founding blacks were either all slaves or, if free, without any national political or legal rights. He declared that blacks:

> are not included, and were not intended to be included, under the word 'citizens' in the Constitution, and can therefore claim none of the rights and privileges which the instrument provides and secures to citizens of the United States. On the contrary, they were at that time [1787] considered as a subordinate and inferior class of beings who had been subjugated by the dominant race, and, whether emancipated or not, yet remained subject to their authority, and had no rights or privileges but such as those who held the power and Government might choose to grant them.

According to Taney blacks were then viewed as "so far inferior, that they had no rights which the white man was bound to respect."[34] Thus, he concluded that blacks could never be citizens of the United States, even if they were born in the country and considered to be citizens of the states in which they lived.

Taney's decision infuriated many northerners, even those who did not believe in racial equality and opposed black suffrage. Republicans around the nation embraced the dissents. Horace Greeley, the Republican editor of the *New York Tribune*, responded to the decision with outrage, calling Taney's opinion "wicked," "atrocious," and "abominable" and a "collation of false statements and shallow sophistries." The paper's editor thought Taney's decision had no more validity than the opinions that might be expressed in any "Washington bar-room." The *Chicago Tribune* declared that Taney's statements on black citizenship were "inhuman dicta."[35] In his famous "House Divided Speech" in 1858, Abraham Lincoln predicted that the Court would soon decide "the next" *Dred Scott* decision, which would force slavery on the North.

Southerners, on the other hand, considered the result to be a great victory for their understanding of the Constitution. South Carolina's *Charleston Daily Courier* cheered the Supreme Court's ruling "that the Missouri Compromise is unconstitutional ... and that free negroes have no rights as citizens, under the Constitution of the United States." The paper's editors "confidently believe[d]" that the decision would "settle these vexed questions forever, quiet the country, and relieve it of abolition agitation, and tend greatly to perpetuate our Union—our Constitutional Union—the greatest political boon ever vouchsafed by God to man." Northern Democrats hoped that the decision would undermine the Republican Party, which had been organized to oppose the spread of slavery into the territories. The official organ of the Buchanan administration, *The Washington Union* happily declared, "the sectional question" was "settled, and that henceforth sectionalism will cease to be a dangerous element in our political contests."[36]

Dred Scott is usually considered to be the worst decision in the nation's history and a cause of the Civil War. It remains a blot on the history of the nation and the Court, but Taney's views may have accurately reflected the proslavery Constitution written in 1787.[37] In response to the decision, the black abolitionist Frederick Douglass displayed remarkable optimism. He told a New York audience, "You will readily ask me how I am affected by this devilish decision—this judicial incarnation of wolfishness! My answer is, and no thanks to the slaveholding wing of the Supreme Court, my hopes were never brighter than now." Douglass believed that the decision would raise "the National Conscience." Moreover, he saw in the decision the beginning of the great cataclysm that could destroy slavery:

> The Supreme Court of the United States is not the only power in this world. It is very great, but the Supreme Court of the Almighty is greater. Judge Taney can do many things, but he cannot perform impossibilities. He cannot bale out the ocean, annihilate this firm old earth, or pluck the silvery star of liberty from our Northern sky. He may decide and decide again; but he cannot reverse the decision of the Most High. He cannot change the essential nature of things—making evil good, and good, evil.[38]

Douglass proved far more prescient than he could have imagined. Less than a decade after the decision, slavery would be abolished and by 1870 the Constitution would be amended to make blacks citizens of the United States with equal political and legal rights. African Americans would serve in Congress and black lawyers would appear before the U.S. Supreme Court. *Dred Scott* would be overturned by war, constitutional amendments, and the tide of history. At the same time, however, history would prove that Douglass was far too optimistic. The racism that led to the decision would remain, and come back to haunt the nation in new forms.

3

Emancipation and Freedom: The Civil War and the Second Founding

etween 1861 and 1870 the U.S. Constitution went through a radical transformation, as did the rest of the nation. The Civil War led to the deaths of more than 650,000 Americans (on both sides of the war) and injuries to millions. The nation spent vast sums on the war and throughout the South farms, houses, workshops, and factories were destroyed. The American South lost immense amounts of wealth and productive capacity. The rest of the nation paid dearly in lives and money for the ultimate victory and the preservation of the Union, but the northern states did not suffer much destruction, and the huge economic stimulus of the war led to new factories and economic development. On balance, the nation probably emerged from the war richer and more productive than it had been when the war began. The national government was stronger than it had ever been, and while it would be weakened after the war, the federal government would never be reduced to its prewar size or its prewar lack of legal and economic power.

The most profound change, of course, took place in the arena of slavery and race. In December 1860 about four million Americans lived in slavery. Five years later slavery had come to a dramatic and abrupt end. All of the slaves were now free. Most of them had found freedom during the course of the war and its immediate aftermath by one of several paths. From almost the beginning of the war slaves near the lines of the U.S. Army abandoned their masters and found freedom and work in Army camps. Congressional action ended slavery in the District of Columbia and the territories. Starting in late 1862 loyal masters freed thousands of slaves who then served in the Army. The Emancipation Proclamation freed millions of slaves in the South, although it took the arrival of the United States Army to effectuate this freedom. Finally, the Thirteenth Amendment, ratified in December 1865, emancipated the remaining slaves in the nation.

Slavery was at the center of the war. Eleven southern states seceded because they feared that the Lincoln Administration threatened slavery. Shortly before the Civil War began, the Confederate vice president, Alexander Stephens of Georgia, publicly declared that slavery was the "cornerstone" of the Confederacy. Initially other Confederate leaders were angry at Stephens's blunt honesty, but within a few weeks the Confederate president, Jefferson Davis, said much the same thing. In his second inaugural address, President Abraham Lincoln recognized this as well, noting, "One-eighth of the whole population were colored slaves, not distributed generally over the Union, but localized in the southern part of it. These slaves constituted a peculiar and powerful interest. All knew that this interest was somehow the cause of the war."[39]

While slavery was the cause of the war, initially Lincoln made no moves against it. Under the Constitution the national government had no power to interfere with slavery in the states. Thus, when Lincoln entered office he could in good conscience assert, as he did in his first inaugural, "I have no purpose, directly or indirectly, to interfere with the institution of slavery in the States where it exists. I believe I have no lawful right to do so, and I have no inclination to do so."[40] Lincoln's goal was to preserve the Constitution, not to violate it by trying to end slavery.

However, once the war began Lincoln's understanding of constitutional limitations, constitutional powers, and constitutional realities changed. While the administration never accepted the legality of secession, it did accept that the collective actions of the Confederate states altered how the Constitution could be applied to the South. Early in the war, Confederate Colonel Charles K. Mallory demanded the return of his slaves who had taken refuge at Fortress Monroe in Virginia. Mallory based his claim on the Constitution and Fugitive Slave Law of 1850. U.S. General Benjamin F. Butler, who had been a lawyer before the war, refused to return the slaves, explaining to that they were "contrabands" of war, while noting "that the fugitive slave act did not affect a foreign country, which Virginia claimed to be and she must reckon it one of the infelicities of her position that in so far at least she was taken at her word." The Lincoln administration did not agree that Virginia was a "foreign country," but in the summer of 1861 the administration adopted Butler's contraband policy.[41]

The following summer Lincoln famously told members of Congress from the loyal slave states that they should urge their state legislatures to end slavery through compensated emancipation funded by Congress, while there was still time to do so. He warned them that the "incidents of war" could "not be avoided" and that "mere friction and abrasion" would destroy slavery. He bluntly predicted slavery "will be gone and you will have nothing valuable in lieu of it."[42] Lincoln did not claim that Congress or the executive branch could end slavery in the loyal states, but the implication was there. By this time Lincoln was comfortable with the idea that on his own he could end slavery in the Confederacy. In September 1862 he told a group of ministers, he had "no objections" to emancipating Confederate slaves "on legal or constitutional grounds," noting that "as commander-in-chief of the army and navy, in time of war, I suppose I have a right to take any measure which may best subdue the enemy."[43]

Thus, when it became clear that a speedy end to the crisis would not occur, Lincoln developed a theory of emancipation, based on his role as commander-in-chief of the Army. It was in that capacity that he issued the Emancipation Proclamation. Emancipation would be a war measure, designed to deprive those in rebellion of the labor of their slaves. It was limited to those places that were under Confederate control because he still had no constitutional power to touch slavery within the loyal states, or even those states or parts of states where the rebellion had subdued the Army.

Having developed a constitutional theory for emancipation, Lincoln did not issue the proclamation until three other preconditions were met. First, he had to be certain emancipation would not push the loyal slave states, especially Kentucky, into the Confederacy. As he told a group of Chicago ministers, a precipitous move against slavery would take "fifty thousand bayonets" from Kentucky out of the United States army and give them to the Confederates.[44] Military success in late 1861 and early 1862, especially General Ulysses S. Grant's capture of Forts Henry and Donelson in northern Tennessee and the fall of two Confederate state capitals, Nashville and Baton Rouge, seemed to ensure that neither Kentucky nor Missouri would join the Confederacy.

Second, Lincoln needed to be certain he had political support to move against slavery. Congressional action against slavery in 1861–62 convinced Lincoln that he could move against bondage. In the First Confiscation Act (1861) Congress provided for the emancipation of some slaves owned by Confederates. In the spring and summer of 1862 Congresses immediately ended slavery in the District of Columbia through compensated emancipation, ended slavery in the territories without compensation (thus ignoring Chief Justice Taney's holding in *Dred Scott* that Congress had no power to do this), prohibited Army officers from returning runaway slaves, and provided for new methods of emancipating slaves owned by Confederates in the Second Confiscation Act. By the late summer of 1862 Lincoln knew he had substantial support in Congress and in much of the North, for moving against slavery.

Finally, Lincoln could not issue an Emancipation Proclamation until it seemed likely that he might win the war. Otherwise, it would be a meaningless and embarrassing stunt. As he told a group of ministers, it would be "like the Pope's bull against the comet." He asked how he "could free the slaves" when he could not "enforce the Constitution in the rebel States."[45] By the time Lincoln made these statements, he was close to issuing the Proclamation, waiting only for a substantial battlefield success, which came a short time later at Antietam.

Lincoln's proclamation was a constitutional innovation—an executive order affecting the personal lives of millions of people. Lincoln worried about its constitutionality, and fully expected it to be challenged in court when the war ended. The challenge would have created a set of theoretical dilemmas. Southerners would have argued that Lincoln was correct in 1861 and the Union was indissoluble. Therefore, the South was never legally out of the Union and thus the national government had no power to take private property without just compensation and due process of law. Clearly, freeing millions of slaves was just that. The Lincoln administration would have argued that taking slaves was a legitimate war measure *because* the slaves were being used to further the aims of the rebellion, and in that sense they were no different than weapons or cavalry horses. This would have been problematic, however, since the same arguments could have been made about all property being used by the South to fight the war. The administration might have argued successfully that once they left the Union the would-be Confederate states had reverted to territories, and that Congress had power to end slavery in the territories—despite the assertions of Chief Justice Taney in *Dred Scott* that Congress did not have this power. But the proclamation did not come from Congress. Even if the courts had upheld the proclamation, it did not affect slavery in the loyal slave states and those parts of the Confederacy, such as all of Tennessee and some counties in Virginia and Louisiana, which were exempted from the reach of the proclamation because they were already deemed to be back under control of the United States. Thus, while revolutionary, the validity of the proclamation was constitutionally uncertain.

The solution was the Thirteenth Amendment, which eliminated most of the problems Lincoln imagined. An amendment could not be declared "unconstitutional," and with sweeping language the amendment solved the problem of ending slavery where the proclamation did not apply. On April 8, 1864, the amendment passed the Senate by a vote of 38–6, which was ten more votes than the required two-thirds. In April it stalled in the House, however, on a vote of 95–66, twelve votes short of the required two-thirds. In December, in the wake of Lincoln's victory in the 1864 election and Republican gains in Congress, Lincoln urged the House to reconsider the amendment. On January 31 the amendment squeaked through the House by a vote of 119–56. The new Congress had not yet taken office, but enough members of the expiring 38th Congress had come to realize that total abolition was inevitable. Illinois ratified the amendment the next day, and by December 15 the required three-quarters of the states had joined Illinois and made the Thirteenth Amendment a part of the Constitution.

Tied to emancipation was a profound change in race relations that had begun to develop during the war. At the beginning of the war thousands of free blacks in the North were prepared to join the Army to fight against the rebellion and the system of slavery that had led to it. But federal law prohibited blacks from serving in the state militias or the Army. The administration still hoped to end the war quickly, believing that the South would come to its senses and return to the Union. Lincoln also had to prevent the secession of the loyal Upper South states. When told by ministers that if he ended slavery he would have God on his side, Lincoln allegedly said, "I would like to have God on my side, but I *need* Kentucky." Like precipitous emancipation, enlisting blacks would probably have pushed Kentucky, and possibly Maryland and Missouri, into the Confederacy. But by the fall of 1862 conditions had changed. With those states firmly in the Union but with the war far from won, Lincoln not only publicly moved against slavery but also allowed the enlistment of black soldiers. By the end of the war more than 200,000 blacks would serve in the Army and Navy. Initially black soldiers were paid less than whites, because of an earlier statute providing for the salaries of civilian blacks working for the military. By 1864 Congress had caught up with changing circumstances and black soldiers were paid the same as whites. Most blacks served under white officers, but a few blacks had been commissioned, and a number, including two of Frederick Douglass's sons, served as noncommissioned officers.[46] Tens of thousands of other blacks worked in military camps as cooks, teamsters, nurses, and in other civilian capacities.

The arming of blacks and their subsequent battlefield sacrifices, successes, and heroism began to alter white perceptions of race. By the end of the war most Republicans favored enfranchising blacks and guaranteeing them political equality. Social equality, however, was more complicated. During the war Congress prohibited segregation by newly chartered streetcar companies in the District of Columbia, but after the war Congress established separate schools for black children in the District.

4

Reconstructing the Union and Remaking the Constitution

he end of the war and the abolition of slavery led to some important rethinking of American race relations, but hardly freed the nation from racist ideology and practice. At the beginning of the war no one imagined black participation in the military or in politics. In his last public speech, Lincoln advocated enfranchising at least some blacks while many in his party were supporting universal adult male suffrage for all Americans, without regard to race. A few progressive politicians, such as Representative Thaddeus Stevens of Pennsylvania, were also beginning to suggest that women should be allowed to vote.

The southern response to defeat, on the other hand, was perhaps predictable, but nevertheless shocking to most northerners. In the fall of 1865 newly elected southern governments passed laws and adopted state constitutional provisions that recognized slavery was over and made adjustments to accommodate the new order. Almost every southern state passed laws to legalize marriages that had taken place under slavery, since those marriages had previously had no status at law. Slave couples could register with county officials and their marriages would be recorded. Children born under slavery were deemed legitimate, as if their parents had been legally married at the time of their birth. Former slaves were also explicitly given the right to sue and be sued and to sign contracts. However, the former Confederate states did their best to undermine black freedom and the ability of former slaves to function in a free market. Some states

---

prohibited former slaves from buying or renting land in towns or buying land in rural areas, thus forcing them to remain agricultural workers. The former slave states restricted their right to testify, banned them from jury service, and denied them the right to vote. Blacks who did not have labor contracts were subject to new vagrancy laws which made them vulnerable to forced labor by "renting" them to planters who would pay their fines. In general, these new laws and constitutional provisions prevented blacks from enjoying their new freedom or gaining an economic foothold in society.

In addition to overt discrimination in the laws, blacks and their white allies in the South faced constant harassment and violence from former Confederates and former slaveholders. Violence was open and blatant. Murders, especially of former slaves, were common and almost never punished.

Most northerners were shocked by these laws and constitutional provisions, as well as the rising tide of white terrorism against blacks, white northerners, and southern white unionists. Having been defeated in battle, and forced to give up slavery, the majority of southern whites seemed as defiant as ever, unwilling to accept the outcome of the war and the necessity of treating blacks as citizens. The reaction to these laws led to the Civil Rights Act of 1866 and later to the Fourteenth Amendment. The prelude to both the act and the constitutional amendment was a massive Congressional investigation by the Joint Committee on Reconstruction.

Report of the Joint Committee on Reconstruction

In December 1865, in response to evidence of southern attempts to impose a new form of servitude on blacks through laws such as those described above, Congress authorized the Joint Committee on Reconstruction to investigate conditions in the South. The joint committee included a number of longtime opponents of slavery and advocates of black rights, including Thaddeus Stevens, John Bingham, George S. Boutwell, and Justin Morrill. The committee's investigations led to the Civil Rights Act of 1866, which Congress passed over President Andrew Johnson's veto on April 9, 1866. On June 13, 1866, Congress passed the Fourteenth Amendment with the necessary two-thirds vote in both houses, and sent it on to the states for ratification.

This was the first time in the history of the nation that Congress focused its attention on the condition of African Americans, and the eight-hundred-page report proved to be a key element in the constitutional revolution that took place between 1865 and 1870. The committee members interviewed scores of people, including recently emancipated slaves, ex-Confederate leaders, former slaveowners, U.S. Army officers, journalists, and others in the South. In its report the committee reminded the nation that the former slaves had "remained true and loyal" throughout the Civil War and "in large numbers, fought on the side of the Union." The committee concluded that it would be impossible to "abandon" the former slaves "without securing them their rights as free men and citizens." Indeed, the "whole civilized world would have cried out against such base ingratitude" if the U.S. government failed to secure and protect the rights of the freedpeople.[47]

The committee also found that southern leaders still "defend[ed] the legal right of secession, and [upheld] the doctrine that the first allegiance of the people is due to the States." Noting the "leniency" of the policies of Congress and the president after the war, which included allowing the former Confederate states to have self-government and not prosecuting the rebels for treason, the committee discovered that "[i]n return for our leniency we receive only an insulting denial of our authority." Rather than accept the outcome of the war, southern whites were using local courts to prosecute loyalists and "Union officers for acts done in the line of official duty." And "similar prosecutions" were "threatened elsewhere as soon as the United States troops [we]re removed."[48]

The committee understood that the task before the Congress and the nation involved three things: preventing former Confederates from reinstating the same type of regime that existed before the war; protecting the liberty of former slaves and guaranteeing them the power to protect their own rights within a new southern political regime; and protecting the rights and safety of white unionists, who were threatened by violence from southern whites who had not accepted the political or social outcome of the war. After investigating the situation in the South, the committee concluded that a constitutional amendment—what became the Fourteenth Amendment—was essential to achieve these goals.

Two categories of evidence were particularly important in setting out the need for civil rights legislation and a constitutional amendment to protect liberty in the states. Congress and the joint committee learned a good deal about conditions in the South by examining statutes and constitutions adopted by former Confederate states that were designed to subjugate the former slaves. The report reprinted some of these legal provisions so the entire nation could understand exactly what was happening in the South. In addition, the joint committee interviewed hundreds of people familiar with conditions in the postwar South. The information from these interviews, along with some published materials, such as excerpts from southern state constitutions, filled the mammoth report. Both the legal documentation and the evidence from interviews led to the inescapable conclusion that the majority of southern whites were not prepared to accept blacks as equal citizens and that many southern whites were willing to use intimidation, violence, and even murder to prevent racial equality in the postwar South.

Southern Black Codes

The southern black codes and constitutions passed in 1865 and 1866 were designed to replicate, as closely as possible, the prewar suppression and exploitation of blacks. The Alabama Black Code of 1865–66 began by acknowledging the new status of blacks, declaring that "[a]ll freedmen, free negroes, and mulattoes" had "the right to sue and be sued, plead and be impleaded." These were rights that slaves had not had. The law also allowed blacks to testify in court, "but only in cases in which freedmen, free negroes and mulattoes" were "parties, either as plaintiff or defendant." In addition, blacks were allowed to testify in prosecutions "for injuries in the persons and property" of blacks. Mississippi enacted similar legislation, which more directly and unambiguously provided that blacks could testify against white criminal defendants only in "prosecutions where the crime charged is alleged to have been committed by a white person upon or against the person or property of a freedman, free negro, or mulatto."[49]

These laws certainly expanded the rights and legal protections of blacks. For the first time in the history of these states, blacks could testify against whites. However, such laws did not give blacks the same legal rights as whites. Under these laws blacks could not testify in a suit between two whites or at the prosecution of a white for harming other whites. Thus, the law in effect declared that blacks were not equal to whites and that their testimony was not as good as that of whites. These restrictions undermined fundamental justice and created dangerous possibilities for free blacks and their white allies. For example, a white suing another white could not use the testimony of a black to support his case. More importantly, under these laws southern white terrorists could kill a white in front of black witnesses, and those witnesses could not testify at the trial. This would undermine the safety of those white teachers, Army officers, Freedmen's Bureau officials, and unionists who supported black rights and the national government.

Thus, while these new laws gave some protection to blacks, the laws did not give them legal equality and did not even fully protect their civil rights.

These laws also undermined the position of the freedmen by giving them the right to enter into contracts and to be sued. Certainly such rights were vital to freedom. But blacks in the Deep South were mostly illiterate, had virtually no experience with either the law or a free economy, and were only a few months out of slavery. They were vulnerable to signing exploitive contracts that committed them to long-term labor agreements. Thus, an Army officer in Texas, Major General Christopher C. Andrews, warned Congress that "[u]nless the freedmen are protected by the government they will be much worse off than when they were slaves" because the whites were prepared "to coerce" blacks into working for unfair wages under unfair contracts.[50]

Other provisions of the black laws more blatantly undermined black freedom. Alabama's law "Concerning Vagrants and Vagrancy" allowed for the incarceration in the public work house of any "laborer or servant who loiters away his time, or refuses to comply with any contract for a term of service without just cause." Mississippi's Civil Rights Act of 1865 provided that if any laborer quit a job before the end of the contract period he would lose all wages earned up to that time. Thus, if a black laborer signed a contract to work for a planter for a year, and left after eleven months, he would get no wages. This allowed employers to mistreat and overwork laborers, knowing they dare not quit. Indeed, a shrewd employer could purposefully make life miserable for workers at the end of a contract term, in hopes that they would quit and forfeit all wages. Mississippi law further declared that any blacks "with no lawful employment or business" would be considered vagrants, and could be fined up to fifty dollars. Any black who could not pay the fine would be forcibly hired out to whoever would pay the fine, thus creating another form of unfree labor. The same act created a one-dollar poll tax for all free blacks. Anyone not paying the tax could also be declared a vagrant and thus assigned to work for a white planter. Other laws also prohibited blacks from renting land or houses in towns or cities, thus in effect forcing blacks into the countryside, where they would be doomed to agricultural labor.

Laws such as these set the stage for a new system of forced labor. Southern states passed these laws just before, or immediately after, the ratification of the Thirteenth Amendment. They were attempts to reduce blacks to a status somewhere between that of slaves (which they no longer were) and full free people (which the white South would not allow). The labor contract laws, the vagrancy laws, and the laws limiting the ability of blacks to rent in urban areas were designed to create a kind of serfdom, tying the former slaves to the land, just as they were once tied to their masters.

The new state constitutions were equally oppressive. The Florida Constitution, for example, limited suffrage to whites and prohibited any person employed by the United States—white or black—from voting in the state unless he was a resident of Florida before entering federal service. The same constitution prohibited blacks from serving as jurors and limited their testimony to cases involving blacks. The Arkansas Constitution likewise limited voting to whites; banned federal officers, whether white or black, from voting; and in other ways discriminated against blacks. The Georgia Constitution was similar, limiting voting to whites. Further, the state used a statute to limit black testimony.[51]

The southern black codes were not the only cause of northern astonishment at southern behavior. Even more important, perhaps, was the violence directed at blacks and their white allies after the war.

Southern Violence

While Congress was debating what would eventually become the Civil Rights Act of 1866 Senator Charles Sumner of Massachusetts received a box containing the finger of a black man. The accompanying note read, "You old son of a bitch, I send you a piece of one of your friends, and if that bill of yours passes I will have a piece of you."[52] While not typical of the mail northerners in Congress received, this box and note illustrated all too well the murderous violence that southern whites were prepared to use to suppress black freedom.

The evidence presented in the massive Committee Report documented the dangers to blacks and white unionists—and the nation itself—posed by the refusal of most former Confederates to accept black freedom. Testimony about the conditions in Tennessee illustrated the dangers for blacks and white unionists in the South. Everyone agreed that Tennessee had more loyal white citizens than any other former Confederate state, and in the end the committee endorsed its immediate readmission to the Union.[53] Nevertheless, a sampling of the testimony gathered from Tennessee supports the understanding that the committee that wrote the Fourteenth Amendment was fully aware of the need for a powerful weapon to force change and protect freedom in the South. Testimony from other states reveals that the rest of the South was even more prone to violence towards blacks and unionists, and that liberty was even more imperiled elsewhere in the former Confederacy.

Major General Edward Hatch testified that whites in much of Tennessee were unwilling to accept black liberty. General Hatch noted that "the negro is perfectly willing to work, but he wants a guarantee that he will be secured in his rights under his contract" and that "his life and property" be "secured." Blacks understood they were "not safe from the poor whites." He noted that whites wanted "some kind of legislation" to "establish a kind of peonage; not absolute slavery but that they can enact such laws as will enable them to manage the negro as they please—to fix the price to be paid for his labor." And, if blacks resisted this reestablishment of bondage, "[t]hey are liable to be shot."

Major General Clinton Fisk, for whom one of the nation's first black colleges, Fisk University, would be named, testified about the murderous nature of former "slaveholders and returned rebel soldiers." Such men "persecute bitterly" the former slaves "and pursue them with vengeance, and treat them with brutality, and burn down their dwellings and school-houses." Fisk pointed out this was "not the rule" everywhere in Tennessee, but nevertheless such conduct existed. And, as everyone understood, Tennessee was the most progressive state on these issues in the former Confederacy.

Lieutenant Colonel R. W. Barnard was less optimistic than General Fisk. Perhaps because he was a field officer, Barnard was more likely to see the day-to-day dangers blacks faced. Asked if it was safe to remove troops from Tennessee, he replied, "I hardly know how to express myself on the subject. I have not been in favor of removing the military. I can tell you what an old citizen, a Union man, said to me. Said he, 'I tell you what, if you take away the military from Tennessee, the buzzards can't eat up the niggers as fast as we'll kill 'em.'" Bernard's point was clear: without the protection of the Army, whites in Tennessee would oppress and murder blacks, because, as he told the Committee, "I know there are plenty of bad men there who would maltreat the negro."

Thus, in Tennessee, where loyal Union men were more common than elsewhere in the South, the dangers to blacks were great. In other states the dangers were extraordinarily greater. Major General John W. Turner reported that in Virginia "all of the [white] people" were "extremely reluctant to grant to the negro his civil rights—those privileges that pertain to freedom, the protection of life, liberty, and property before the laws, the right to testify in courts, etc." Turner noted that whites were "reluctant even to consider and treat the negro as a free man, to let him have his half of the sidewalk or the street crossing." They would only "concede" such rights to blacks "if it is ever done, because they are forced to do it." He noted that poor whites were "disposed to ban the negro, to kick him and cuff him, and threaten him." A white Virginia farmer, George B. Smith, testified that whites in the state, "maltreat [blacks] every day" and that blacks had "[n]ot a particle" of a chance "to obtain justice in the civil courts of Virginia." Smith told the committee that a black or "a Union man" had as much chance of obtaining justice in Virginia as "a rabbit would in a den of lions." Others in Virginia explained, over and over again, how the whites were trying to reduce blacks to servitude with laws and violence. The white sheriff of Fairfax County noted that the state was "passing laws" to "disfranchise" black voters and "passing vagrant laws on purpose to oppress the colored people and to keep them in vassalage, and doing everything they can to bring back things of their old condition, as near as possible."

U.S. District Judge John C. Underwood, who had lived in Virginia since the 1840s, described the cold-blooded murder of a white unionist by a returning Confederate medical officer. The state did not prosecute anyone for the crime. He also noted that the murderer of an Army officer had "not yet been punished" but was "still at large." He believed that white unionists in Virginia were even more vulnerable than blacks, because the Army would intercede to protect the freedmen, while "a Union man could" not "expect to obtain justice in the courts of the State." But, if the Army abandoned the state and left the fate of the freedmen to the native whites of Virginia the situation would be radically altered. Judge Underwood quoted a "most intelligent" man from Alexandria, who declared that "sooner than see the colored people raised to a legal and political equality, the southern people would prefer their total annihilation."

A U.S. Army captain stationed in North Carolina described how a black man was shot down in cold blood near Camden. He reported "numerous cases" of the "maltreatment of blacks," including flogging and shooting, and that "instances of cruelty were numerous" and predicted that without U.S. troops schoolhouses for blacks would be burned and teachers harassed. A minister in Goldsborough, North Carolina, reported the cold-blooded shooting of a black in order to take his horse. When another former slave led soldiers to the culprit, this black man was also murdered. Lieutenant Colonel Dexter H. Clapp told the committee about a gang of North

Carolina whites who "first castrated" and then "murdered" a black, but that when the culprits escaped from jail the local police refused to even attempt to capture them. This gang then shot "several negroes." One of these men, a wealthy planter, later killed a twelve-year-old black boy and wounded another. A local police sergeant "brutally wounded a freedman ... in his custody." While the man's arms were tied behind his back, the policeman struck him on the back of his head with a gun. It was later shown that this man had "committed no offence whatever." This policeman later "whipped another freedman" so that "from his neck to his hips his back was one mass of gashes." The policeman left the bleeding man outside all night. A black who defended himself when assaulted by a white was given twenty-two lashes with a whip over a two-hour period, then "tied up by his thumbs for two hours, his toes touching the ground only," then "given nine more lashes and then tied up by his thumbs for another two hours." A planter in the same area whipped two black women until their backs were "a mass of gashes." Clapp asserted that away from military posts "scenes like these" were "frequent occurrences" in "portions" of North Carolina.

Major General Rufus Saxton, a West Point graduate, reported that in Edgefield, South Carolina, local whites treated free people as if they were slaves. One "freedman [and] three children, two male and one female, were stripped naked, tied up, and whipped severely," while a woman was given a hundred lashes while tied to a tree. Another man was whipped with a stick, while two children were also whipped. Saxton reported shootings, whippings, various forms of torture, whipping of naked women, floggings, and beatings of all kinds. In addition to attacks on blacks by individual planters, ruffians, and gangs, Saxton reported a more ominous trend: "organized bands of 'regulators'—armed men—who make it their business to traverse these counties, and maltreat negroes without any avowedly definite purpose in view. They treat the negroes, in many instances, in the most horrible and atrocious manner, even to maiming them cutting their ears off, etc."

General George Armstrong Custer reported that whites in Texas blamed the black man for "their present condition," and thus they did not "hesitate" to use "every opportunity to inflict injuries upon him in order, seemingly, to punish him for this." Custer reported "it is of a weekly, if not of daily, occurrence that freedmen are murdered. Their bodies are found in different parts of the country," but no whites were ever charged, even when they were known. Custer reported that "[c]ases have occurred of white men meeting freedmen they never saw before, and murdering them merely from this feeling of hostility to them as a class." On the other hand, Custer noted that blacks were routinely convicted and jailed for minor offenses. Testimony from the rest of the South mirrored the violence and denial of rights sketched out here as the committee heard numbing accounts of blacks being beaten, maimed, and killed, as well as just disappearing.

Perhaps even more horrible than the fear of violence was the threat of re-enslavement. Brigadier General Charles H. Howard, the brother of war hero Major General Oliver Otis Howard, reported instances in Georgia of blacks being held on plantations against their will and of others being kidnapped and taken to Cuba, where slavery was still legal. At South Newport, Georgia, a woman escaped from the plantation of her former master "after much maltreatment." She reported that her former master had "insisted that she and her children were not free, [and] that he cared nothing for 'Lincoln's proclamation.'" When she insisted on leaving "she was confined on bread and water" until she escaped. However, she was forced to leave her children behind. Howard also reported that at New Altamaha, Georgia, Army officers had investigated "a case where certain parties were charged with kidnapping colored children and shipping them to Cuba." Two children "mysteriously disappeared" but were then found in Florida after their former owner was placed "under bonds to produce the children." The former owner could not explain how the children got to Florida, or how he knew where they were. The implication was clear: the former master had kidnapped the children, sent them (or took them) to Florida, and was preparing to send them to Cuba where they could be sold as slaves.

The Civil Rights Act of 1866 and the Fourteenth Amendment

The committee report presented massive evidence of legal discrimination, racial violence, and the refusal of southern states and local governments to protect the most basic rights of blacks or to protect the lives of former slaves, southern white unionists, and northerners helping rebuild the South. In response to this evidence the committee drafted the Civil Rights Act of 1866, the first federal law ever designed to protect the liberties of American citizens. The law declared that all persons born in the United States were citizens of the nation and that "such citizens, of every race and color, without regard to any previous condition of slavery or involuntary servitude ... shall have the same right, in every State and Territory in the United

States, to make and enforce contracts, to sue, be parties and give evidence, to inherit, purchase, lease, sell, hold, and convey real and personal property, and to full and equal benefit of all laws and proceedings for the security of person and property, as is enjoyed by white citizens, and shall be subject to like punishment, pains, and penalties, and to none other, any law, statute, ordinance, regulation, or custom, to the contrary notwithstanding."[54] The law empowered the president to use the Army and Navy, as well as state militias, to protect the civil rights of all Americans. In this respect it mirrored the Fugitive Slave Law of 1850, in which Congress had authorized the use of the military to capture and return runaway slaves. President Andrew Johnson, a former slave owner who had deep hostility to black civil rights, vetoed this bill, as he had the Freedmen's Bureau Bill. Congress overrode both vetoes.

Congress passed the Civil Rights Act under the enforcement powers of the Thirteenth Amendment. The act was designed to remove the badges of slavery and end discrimination associated with slavery. But some supporters of the act, especially Representative John Bingham of Ohio, worried that the Thirteenth Amendment did not give Congress such broad authority. He thus pushed for the Fourteenth Amendment, which Congress passed in 1866 and the states ratified in 1868.

The Fourteenth Amendment was the most complicated and far-reaching amendment ever added to the Constitution. It contained five sections, but most scholarship and most litigation has focused on Section 1, which addressed citizenship, prohibitions on discrimination, and limitations on state infringement of individual rights and Section 5, which gave Congress power to enforce the amendment. Before turning to Section 1, a brief examination of Sections 2, 3, and 4 is in order.

The abolition of slavery led to an ironic and unexpected result: the South's congressional representation would increase, because the former slaves could now be counted fully for purposes of representation. However, at the time, free blacks were not allowed to vote in any of the former slave states. A simple solution to this problem would have been the enfranchisement of free blacks—what Congress ultimately did when it sent the Fifteenth Amendment to the states for ratification. But, consistent with existing notions of federalism, Congress was reluctant to directly interfere with the rights of the states to set rules for voting. In addition, most northern states did not allow blacks to vote. Thus, an amendment prohibiting race discrimination in voting might not have been ratified. With these two issues in mind, Congress wrote Section 2 of the amendment, which allowed for the reduction of the number of representatives a state received if the state did not grant universal adult male suffrage. If Congress had actually implemented this provision either the South would have had to give blacks the right to vote on the same basis as whites *or* the southern states would have lost significant numbers of representatives in Congress. The subsequent history of race relations in the nation might have been dramatically different if the clause had been enforced. But it was not. Instead, Congress acquiesced in the wide disfranchisement of blacks late in the century. In 1890 Congressman Henry Cabot Lodge of Massachusetts, with the encouragement of President Benjamin Harrison, managed to get a bill enforcing this clause through the House, only to see it die in the Senate.[55]

Section 3 of the amendment limited the office holding potential of former Confederate leaders, but this provision had relatively little effect on politics, as many former Confederates were given exemptions. Moreover, as they aged, their children and grandchildren took their place in fighting against racial equality in the South. Section 4 was the most straightforward and successful provision of the amendment. It prevented any former master from making a claim for compensation for the emancipation of slaves and prohibited the southern states from paying off Confederate debts.

If Section 4 was the most straightforward, Section 1 was the most complicated and problematic. Its meaning remains contested a century and a half after it was written, even though it is also one of the most important provisions of the Constitution. Section 1 provides that

> All persons born or naturalized in the United States, and subject to the jurisdiction thereof, are citizens of the United States and of the State wherein they reside. No State shall make or enforce any law which shall abridge the privileges or immunities of citizens of the United States; nor shall any State deprive any person of life, liberty, or property, without due process of law; nor deny to any person within its jurisdiction the equal protection of the laws.

The first sentence of this section was a revolutionary change in the nature of citizenship in the United States. Most obviously, it overturned the holding in *Dred Scott* that native-born blacks could never be citizens of the United States. Under the Fourteenth Amendment all African Americans who had been born in the United States were now American citizens and citizens of the states where they lived.

This sentence also had implications for other minorities. At the time, federal law only allowed white immigrants to become naturalized citizens of the United States. None of the Chinese immigrants in California and Oregon were eligible for citizenship at this time, and under *Dred Scott* their American-born children could not have been American citizens because Chief Justice Taney clearly held that American citizenship was limited to that class of people—whites—who he asserted were citizens at the founding. Indeed, in *Dred Scott* Taney asserted that the 1790 naturalization act "shows that citizenship at that time [the founding] was perfectly understood to be confined to the white race; and that they alone constituted the sovereignty in the Government."[56] In his concurring opinion Justice Daniel also used the naturalization act to support the argument that only whites could be citizens of the nation because Congress had "restricted that boon to free white aliens alone."[57] Taney did not discuss the status of people from Asia in *Dred Scott*, but he made it clear throughout the opinion that *only* white people could ever be citizens of the United States. Over and over again he asserted that blacks and Indians could *never* be citizens of the United States. If blacks and Indians who could vote and hold office in Massachusetts or Maine could not be considered citizens of the United States, then there was no reason to believe that the American-born children of Asian immigrants in California or Oregon—who could not vote, hold office, or even testify against whites—could somehow be considered natural-born citizens of the United States. *Dred Scott* emphatically stood for the principle that citizenship was based on the original intent of the Founders and that, as Taney explained, their intent was that only white people could be citizens of the United States. Indeed, Taney declared, "This opinion was at that time fixed and universal in the civilized portion of the white race. It was regarded as an axiom in morals as well as in politics, which no one thought of disputing."[58]

While the West Coast states *could* have given *state* citizenship to the American-born children of Chinese immigrants, they were certainly under no obligation to do so, and it was unlikely they would. In the 1860s California and Oregon discriminated against Chinese in a variety of ways and would continue to do so until after World War II, while expanding their discrimination to include Japanese and other Asian immigrants and their American-born children. But, under the Fourteenth Amendment, at least the American-born children of Asian immigrants, like blacks, would be U.S. citizens. The first sentence of the Fourteenth Amendment clearly gave state and national citizenship to the American-born children of Chinese immigrants.[59] And in *United States v. Wong Kim Ark* (1898) the U.S. Supreme Court so held.

The second sentence of Section 1 of the amendment contained the elements of a constitutional revolution that would affect all Americans both at the time and in the future. The first clause of this sentence is the most ambiguous: "No State shall make or enforce any law which shall abridge the privileges or immunities of citizens of the United States." Many scholars believe that this sentence was designed to apply some of the Bill of Rights to the states. Presumably, the "privileges or immunities" of United States citizenship included the rights to freedom of speech, religion, assembly, and protections from warrantless searches and arrests. These rights also included a right to travel and pass undisturbed from one state to another. Before the Civil War the southern states had uniformly denied free blacks an unencumbered right to travel and of course had also denied slaves such a right. The slave states had also denied freedom of speech and assembly to blacks and also to whites if they challenged the legitimacy of slavery. In the 1850s the most popular book in the United States was *Uncle Tom's Cabin*, but in much of the South it was illegal to even own this book. Free speech simply did not exist in the antebellum South for anyone—white or black—who opposed slavery. After the Civil War former slaves, black veterans, northern whites, and southern unionists faced discrimination and physical danger throughout the South. As the Joint Committee on Reconstruction, which wrote the Fourteenth Amendment, learned from the testimony of one Virginian, a black or "a Union man" had as much chance of obtaining justice in Virginia as "a rabbit would in a den of lions." This was true for the other former Confederate states as well. At the time most people believed that the privileges and immunities clause of the Fourteenth Amendment would cure at least part of this problem. But in *The Slaughter-House Cases* (1873) the Supreme Court would eviscerate the clause, holding that it was not the intention of the framers of this amendment "to transfer the security and protection of all the civil rights" of United States citizens "from the States to the Federal government."[60] Indeed, in that case the Court would hold that this clause of the Fourteenth Amendment had almost no operational meaning at all.

The second clause—"nor shall any State deprive any person of life, liberty, or property, without due process of law"—was also designed to protect the fundamental liberties and rights of free blacks as well as unionists in the South. Oddly, this clause was not the subject of litigation in civil rights cases in the decade after the war. It remained basically ignored by the Court as a source of fundamental political liberties, legal protections, and civil rights until the twentieth century. The nineteenth- and early twentieth-century Court did apply the clause to protect economic interests from state regulation. Two generations later, however, in *Gitlow v. New York* (1925) the Court would conclude that "due process" prohibited the states from abridging freedom of speech. The court held that the term due process "incorporated" the free speech clause of the First Amendment against the states.[61] Following *Gitlow* the Court gradually used incorporation to apply most of the protections of the Bill of Rights to the states. In the mid-twentieth century such incorporation would help protect civil rights demonstrators and newspapers reporting about civil rights. Incorporation would also apply most of the criminal due process provisions of the Fourth, Fifth, Sixth, and Eighth Amendments against the states, which would be particularly important in protecting African Americans from discrimination in criminal trials in the South.

The last clause of Section 1—"nor deny to any person within its jurisdiction the equal protection of the laws"—should have made almost all forms of state-mandated segregation unconstitutional. However, in the nineteenth century the Court never interpreted the clause in this way. Instead, the Court accepted race distinctions that were "neutral" or that provided for equal treatment through separate facilities. Thus, the Court would uphold bans on interracial marriage on the theory that the law treated whites and blacks equally: whites could not marry blacks and blacks could not marry whites. Similarly, the Court in *Plessy v. Ferguson* (1896) would uphold laws requiring the separation of blacks and whites on railroad cars on the theory that "separate but equal" facilities gave everyone "equal protection of the laws." In the 1930s and 1940s the courts would begin to require that southern states actually provide equal facilities, including equal pay for teachers. Eventually, in the 1950s and 1960s the Court would interpret this clause to mean that legally enforced separation of the races was unconstitutional. By the end of the 1960s the Court had found that virtually all forms of race-based discrimination were unconstitutional.

The Fifteenth Amendment and Voting

In February 1869 Congress passed what became the Fifteenth Amendment, which was ratified on March 30, 1870. Section 1 provided that the "right of citizens of the United States to vote shall not be denied or abridged by the United States or by any state on account of race, color, or previous condition of servitude." Section 2 gave Congress the "power to enforce this article by appropriate legislation." The amendment was in part a compromise, because radicals in Congress wanted to prohibit literacy tests for voting but could not get enough support for such a clause. For similar reasons the amendment did not prohibit racial tests for office holding. The amendment was a blend of racial egalitarianism and practical politics. Moderate Republicans wanted to make sure that former slaves in the South would continue to be able to vote and support the Party of Lincoln. Starting in the 1890s southern white majorities would take advantage of the narrow language of the amendment by using poll taxes, literacy tests, and complicated registration and voting procedures to disfranchise almost all southern blacks.

Many northern supporters of civil rights concluded that with this amendment the abolitionist and egalitarian revolution was complete. Blacks were now equal citizens and could actively participate in politics to protect their new freedom. In the South, however, continued violence from the Ku Klux Klan and other white terrorist organizations demonstrated that constitutional amendments were insufficient to secure black liberty and political equality. By 1871 Congress acting under the enforcement provisions of all three new amendments, had passed three laws, known as the Force Acts and the Ku Klux Klan Act, to suppress white terrorism. The combined efforts of the Army and federal prosecutions undermined the Ku Klux Klan for a while, and by the mid-1870s blacks were able to vote in large numbers. But violence and intimidation were never far from the surface of southern politics, and at no time were former slaves truly free to participate in politics or the economy without fear of violence. Shortly after the death of its sponsor, Senator Charles Sumner of Masschusetts, Congress passed the Civil Rights Act of 1875. Acting under the enforcement provisions of the Fourteenth Amendment, Congress prohibited discrimination in public accommodations and public transportation, such as hotels, restaurants, theaters, and street cars. This would be the last civil rights act passed by Congress until after World War II.

5

From Reconstruction to Jim Crow: The Betrayal of the Constitution

he election of 1876 was one of the most controversial in American history. Democrats claimed that Republicans in the Deep South stuffed ballot boxes and miscounted votes. Republicans argued that the Democrats used intimidation, violence, threats, and fraud to prevent tens of thousands of southern blacks from voting. Ultimately Congress, on a purely partisan vote, certified Republican electors in the contested southern states, leading to the election of Rutherford B. Hayes, a minor Civil War hero who was personally committed to black equality. The compromise that brought Hayes to the White House, however, included the withdrawal of the last federal troops from the South and the formal end of Reconstruction. Hayes would appoint John Marshall Harlan to the Supreme Court—the most committed supporter of civil rights to sit on the Court until the mid-twentieth century. But Harlan's support of civil rights would be lonely. He often dissented, while the Court, in case after case, undermined the new amendments and the Reconstruction era laws passed to protect black civil rights.

The dismantling of Reconstruction began before the 1876 election. For the most part it was led by a Supreme Court that was deeply unsympathetic to the extraordinary changes that had taken place in the nation between 1861 and 1870. Most of the justices were not hostile to black freedom per se. They were, after all, mostly Republicans, sent to the Court by Lincoln and Grant. But most of them were never able to fully accept that the Civil War and the three new constitutional amendments had radically altered federalism and the relationship of the national government to the rights of the citizens. They had come of age at a time when the Bill of Rights was a set of limitations on the national government, while the states were free to regulate fundamental liberties as they wished. Moreover, with the exception of Justice Harlan, who was from Kentucky, the justices never fully understood the deep hatred that most southern whites had for free blacks. Nor did they appreciate the violence of the postwar South or the necessity of using the new amendments and statutes to protect both black freedom and the physical safety of the former slaves and their few white allies in the South.

The Court and Racial Violence

The narrow vision of the Court first appeared in *Blyew v. United States* (1872). Blyew and another white man had murdered four blacks in Kentucky. All of the witnesses to the crime were blacks, but Kentucky law prohibited blacks from testifying against whites. Thus, the U.S. attorney moved the case to federal court, believing that justice could only be done in that forum, where black witnesses had been able to testify since the end of the war. The U.S. attorney acted under the Civil Rights Act of 1866, which provided that the "District Courts shall, concurrently with the Circuit Courts, have cognizance of all causes, civil and criminal, affecting persons who are denied or cannot enforce in the courts or judicial tribunals of the State or locality where they may be, any of the rights secured to them by the first section of this act." The defendants were convicted of murder in U.S. District Court and appealed. The Supreme Court overturned the conviction. Justice Strong concluded that the "rights" protected by the act were only those of the litigants in a case, not the rights of excluded witnesses or other third parties, nor even the victim of a crime, since victims of crime are not parties to the prosecution of the perpetrators. Since *Blyew* was not a case where a black *litigant* or defendant was denied fair process by the state courts, the statute did not apply. In the view of the Supreme Court the "cause" did not include the black victims or the black witnesses, who were prohibited, under Kentucky law, from testifying against whites. Taking a narrow view of who might be affected by the law's enforcement, Strong declared,

> We need hardly add that the jurisdiction of the Circuit Court is not sustained by the fact averred in the indictment that Lucy Armstrong, the person murdered, was a citizen of the African race, and for that reason denied the right to testify in the Kentucky courts. In no sense can she be said to be affected by the cause. Manifestly the act refers to persons in existence. She was the victim of the frightful outrage which gave rise to the cause, but she is beyond being affected by the cause itself.[62]

In dissent, Justice Bradley argued that the position of the Court was "too narrow, too technical, and too forgetful of the liberal objects" of the 1866 act. Bradley stated that the act was a "legitimate consequence" of the Thirteenth Amendment. He wrote, "Merely striking off the fetters of the slave, without removing the incidents and consequences of slavery, would hardly have been a boon to the colored race. Hence, also, the amendment abolishing slavery was supplemented by a clause giving Congress power to enforce it by appropriate legislation." He argued that Section 2 of the amendment, the enforcement section, includes the power to protect the lives and safety of former slaves. He moved to use the "power to do away with the incidents and consequences of slavery, and to instate the freedmen in the full enjoyment of that civil liberty and equality which the abolition of slavery meant."[63] This decision meant that whites could openly attack and kill former slaves with little fear that they could be prosecuted in a federal court.

A year later, in *The Slaughter-House Cases*, Justice Miller asserted that the privileges and immunities clause of the amendment did not protect the basic civil rights or civil liberties of all Americans, but only prevented the states from abridging a limited, narrow set of "federal" rights, which Miller refused to define. The case involved the regulation of slaughterhouses in New Orleans, and the Court might have easily held that this sort of public health issue had nothing to do with fundamental liberties under the Fourteenth Amendment. Instead, however, Miller offered a long discussion of the privileges and immunities clause of the Fourteenth Amendment, basically concluding that it had very little substantive meaning, and that the protection of fundamental liberties, like free speech or fair trials, was not protected by the Fourteenth Amendment. Thus, Miller left the fate of the recently emancipated slaves and their white allies largely in the hands of southern state governments, which were being taken over by former Confederates, ex-slaveowners, and their heirs. For Miller, this view was the only option; otherwise, he believed, the Court would become "a perpetual censor upon all legislation of the states, on the civil rights of their own citizens."[64] The dissenters, on the other hand, believed that the amendment had in fact given the Court at least some power over state legislation, in order to guarantee that all Americans would have the same fundamental liberties without regard to what state they lived in. In the mid-twentieth century the Court would come to assume this role as it struck down state laws that discriminated on the basis of race and sometimes age, gender, and even economic status.

In *United States v. Reese* (1876) the Court struck down a portion of the Enforcement Act of 1870, which Congress had passed to implement the Fifteenth Amendment. In this case Reese, a Kentucky election official, had refused to count the votes of blacks in an election. Speaking for an eight to one majority, Chief Justice Morrison Waite held that the act was unconstitutional with the implausible argument that one section of the law banned discrimination based on race, but another section did not. In dissent, Justice Ward Hunt pointed out that in fugitive slave cases, such as *Prigg v. Pennsylvania* (1842) and *Ableman v. Booth* (1859), the antebellum Court had given the Congress great latitude to enforce the fugitive slave clause of the Constitution. Hunt now wanted to protect freedom with the same jurisprudence that had once been used to support slavery. But, the rest of the Court had no interest in this kind of intellectual consistency or in applying the new amendments to states to preserve freedom and equality.

On the same day the Court overturned Reese's conviction, in *United States v. Cruikshank* (1876) the Court reversed the convictions of white terrorists who had attacked a political rally in Louisiana and killed more than one hundred blacks in what is known as the Colfax Massacre. Cruikshank and other whites had been prosecuted under the Force Act of 1871 (also known as the Ku Klux Klan Act), which had been passed to suppress the Ku Klux Klan and prevent precisely the kind of political and racial violence perpetrated by these terrorists. The Court ignored all of the facts of the case and the large number of people killed and instead focused on some minor technical irregularities in the indictments. In doing this, the Court also ignored an 1872 act that specifically directed courts not to overturn convictions in such cases on these minor procedural issues, unless the procedural problems prejudiced the defendants. No one argued that Cruikshank and his co-defendants had been harmed by these technical irregularities. The Court went through each count of the indictment, searching out whatever technical or linguistic problems it could find in order to overturn the conviction. The Court asserted that the crimes committed in Louisiana were violations of state laws and should be tried by the state. However, it was utterly unrealistic to think that the state could in fact prosecute the perpetrators of the crime or that a jury—which at this time would almost certainly have been made up of white men—would have convicted the defendants.

In essence, the Court rejected the idea that the Civil War amendments provided substantive protection for former slaves and that the enforcement clause in each of the amendments allowed the national government to protect the civil rights of individuals. The Court denied that the victims in this case had any federal right to assemble. The Court did not believe that the mob had denied any constitutional rights of the blacks who were killed, wounded, or intimidated. As it had in *The Slaughter-House Cases*, the Court once again read the Civil War amendments as narrowly as possible, preventing the national government from protecting the rights and liberties of former slaves.

Decided in the spring of 1876, *Reese* and *Cruikshank* provided encouragement to southern whites who terrorized blacks during the election that fall. The cases in effect gave whites a green light to intimidate black voters, refuse to count their votes, and even murder blacks who tried to organize politically. After 1876 there would still be some successful civil rights prosecutions in the lower courts, some private lawsuits in which civil rights litigants won, and one Supreme Court victory in a voting case in *Ex parte Yarbrough* (discussed below). However, with a few minor exceptions involving jury discrimination, the late nineteenth-century Court remained hostile to civil rights claims brought under the Reconstruction amendments.

The Court and the Emergence of Segregation: *Hall v. DeCuir*

With the end of Reconstruction the Court faced a resurgence of white supremacy in the South, aimed at segregating blacks and removing them from any positions of public life. The process of segregation took about twenty-five years, and while the impetus came from white southerners, the Court was a willing collaborator in this process.

The first case the Court heard involved an attempt to create an integrated society. During Reconstruction the Louisiana legislature had prohibited common carriers such as steamboats and railroads from segregating passengers by providing that "[a]ll persons shall enjoy equal rights and privileges upon any conveyance of any public character."[65] In 1869 another state law allowed anyone who was segregated, in violation of this act, to sue for damages. When a ship captain refused to allow Josephine DeCuir, an African American woman, to occupy a cabin on his boat she sued and won $1,000. The Louisiana law applied only to public conveyances within the state and DeCuir had attempted to travel only within the state. Nevertheless, ignoring the statute and the facts of the case, the Court focused on the fact that the ship's own destination was ultimately out of state to hold that this law imposed a burden on interstate commerce in violation of the commerce clause of the Constitution. Congress had in fact never passed legislation on this issue and presumably the Fourteenth Amendment allowed, or even required, the states to adopt such laws. However, the Court argued that because many steamboats on the Mississippi passed from state to state, this law placed an undue burden on such shipping.

The Court might easily have concluded that the 1869 statute was nothing more than an implementation of the new amendment. The Court might also have noted that it was the neighboring states, like Mississippi, that violated the commerce clause by *requiring* segregation, rather than Louisiana, which was trying to implement the Fourteenth Amendment. Had the Court strictly followed *DeCuir*, it would have subsequently struck down state laws requiring segregation, leaving it entirely up to the private carriers how they would handle the issue. But this did not happen. In fact, the Court would later uphold state laws requiring segregation on common carriers in *Louisville, New Orleans, and Texas Pacific Railroad v. Mississippi* (1890) and *Plessy v. Ferguson* (1896). *Hall v. DeCuir* remained good law until the Court effectively overturned it in *Morgan v. Virginia* (1946), which struck down state laws requiring segregation in interstate common carriers.

Race and Jury Trials

On March 1, 1880, the Supreme Court decided three cases involving race and jury trials. In *Strauder v. West Virginia* (1880) the Court overturned the murder conviction of a former slave, on the grounds that blacks were excluded from serving on juries in that state. The relevant state law provided that, "All white male persons who are twenty-one years of age and who are citizens of this State shall be liable to serve as jurors."[66]

Speaking for the Court, Justice William Strong noted that this case was "important" because the issues "demand a construction of the recent amendments of the Constitution." Justice Strong concluded that the Civil War amendments had "a common purpose, namely: securing to a race recently emancipated, a race that through many generations had been held in slavery, all the civil rights that the superior race enjoy." Because in the South "discriminations against them [blacks] had been habitual," the new amendments, especially the Fourteenth, were adopted to protect former slaves from "unfriendly action in the States where they were resident." Strong emphatically asserted that the amendment was "designed to assure to the colored race the enjoyment of all the civil rights that under the law are enjoyed by white persons, and to give to that race the protection of the General Government in that enjoyment, whenever it should be denied by the States." Given these conclusions, the Court easily found that a state could not use race as a basis for serving on a jury.[67]

The original defendants in *Virginia v. Rives*, decided at the same time as *Strauder*, were less fortunate. The case involved two black teenagers charged with murder in state court. They were indicted by a grand jury that had no blacks, and tried by a jury that was also entirely white. Consequently, Alexander Rives, the U.S. District Judge, had the case removed to federal court under a federal law that allowed for such removal when a defendant "is denied or cannot enforce in the judicial tribunals of the State ... any right secured to him by any law providing for the equal civil rights of citizens of the United States." Virginia then took the case to the U.S. Supreme Court, arguing that Judge Rives had no right to interfere with the state's criminal justice system. Narrowly reading the law and virtually ignoring the facts of the case, the Court sided with Virginia because, unlike in *Strauder*, Virginia law did not have a statute that specifically prohibited blacks from serving on juries. Speaking for the Court, Justice Strong admitted that the county officials may have purposely refused to call blacks for jury service, but Strong said this fact could not be used to take the case away from Virginia. Rather, Strong suggested that instead the state or the federal government might prosecute the state official for his "criminal misuse of the state law."[68] Strong's decision left the defendants with no remedy for what may have been an unfair conviction, even if it raised the possibility of punishment for the responsible official.

In the third case, *Ex parte Virginia and J. D. Coles*, the Court upheld the federal prosecution of Virginia judge, J. D. Coles, for refusing to allow blacks to serve on grand juries and petit (trial) juries. This prosecution was based on an 1875 federal law that prohibited discrimination on the basis of race or previous condition of servitude in the choosing of jurors. Judge Coles argued that the Fourteenth Amendment and the federal law could only regulate state action, not his individual acts. The Court accepted this understanding of the amendment, but Justice Strong found that a "State acts by its legislative, its executive, or its judicial authorities. It can act in no other way." Therefore, the laws passed to implement the amendment could reach state officials acting in their official capacities to deny rights to African Americans. Strong denied that the federal government lacked power to punish a state judge for his official acts. Rather, he asserted that the 1875 act could reach any public official—"court-criers, tipstaves, sheriffs" and in this case a judge who prevented blacks from serving on juries.[69]

The *Rives* and *Coles* cases created an ironic and almost absurd result. Blacks could be prosecuted by entirely segregated grand and trial juries—they might even be executed after such unfair trials—but they would have no remedy in federal courts to gain a fair trial. The state officials who administered such miscarriages of justice could subsequently be tried and jailed for their behavior. But, even if those responsible for denying blacks fair trials went to jail, the blacks convicted would have no opportunity to get fair trials in their own cases. These cases provided a mixed and confusing understanding of what freedom and racial equality meant under the Constitution. They made it clear that any formal discrimination against blacks in the jury process was not acceptable. But, the Court also indicated that it would allow informal discrimination, even if blatant. After this case, it became increasingly difficult for the federal government to protect black defendants from the harsh justice of the post-Reconstruction South. On the other hand, the expansive interpretation of the Fourteenth Amendment in *Ex parte Virginia and J. D. Coles* offered the possibility of significant protection for black rights *if* the federal government was willing to prosecute white officials for discrimination. Unfortunately, rather than being a precedent for vigorous civil rights enforcement in the future, the case was quickly forgotten and not followed.

The confusing jurisprudence continued for one more term. In *Neal v. Delaware* (1881) the court overturned the conviction of William Neal, an African American, who had been convicted of raping a white woman. No blacks served on either the grand jury that indicted him or the petit jury that convicted him. Under the precedents in *Rives* this should not have mattered. Unlike West Virginia, in the *Strauder* case, Delaware law did not specifically bar blacks from juries. However, Justice Harlan, speaking for the Court, found that this case was essentially like *Strauder* because "in fact, persons of that race, though otherwise qualified, have always, in that County and State, been excluded, because of their color; from service on juries."[70] Jury service in Delaware was tied to being a registered voter and the Delaware Constitution of 1831 restricted voting to "free white male citizens." Neal successfully argued that although blacks could vote in Delaware under the Fifteenth Amendment to the Constitution, the Delaware authorities apparently still applied their state constitution's voter qualifications to jury service. The state denied this charge, asserting that the Fourteenth and Fifteenth Amendments had made the discriminatory clause in the state constitution inoperable. However, the record showed that no black had ever served on jury in Delaware, which clearly undermined the state's claim that it was not discriminating against blacks in choosing juries. In reversing Neal's conviction, Harlan reaffirmed the holding in *Virginia v. Rives* (1880), that a black "cannot claim, as a matter of right, that his race shall have a representation on a jury in a particular case,"[71] but the Court also held that the wholesale exclusion of blacks from juries violated the Constitution.

Neal, like *Strauder* and *Ex parte Virginia*, changed little. In *In re Wood* (1891) the Court would reconfirm that blacks had no right to have members of their race on juries, and thus the federal courts would not overturn convictions on the basis of bias in the choosing of juries as long as there was no statute leading to discrimination, as there had been *Strauder*. In the 1890s the southern states found new ways to prevent blacks from serving on juries without violating the doctrines in *Neal* and *Strauder*, and the Court would accept these more sophisticated methods of discrimination. The Court's attitude became clear at the end of the century, when states disfranchised blacks through subterfuges, like literacy tests. Mississippi, for example, never formally disfranchised blacks, and never formally barred them from jury service. Instead, in 1890 the state introduced a literacy test that state election officials used to disfranchise almost all blacks in the state. Once they could no longer vote, blacks were also effectively barred from jury service. In *Williams v. Mississippi* (1898) the Court refused to interfere with the murder conviction and death sentence of Henry Williams even though there had only been whites on the juries that indicted and convicted him. The Court held that blacks were not barred from voting or jury service because the literacy tests were legitimate bars for voting and not discriminatory, since whites as well as blacks might be prohibited from voting and jury service.

Thus, by the end of the century most of the South had found constitutionally permissible ways to remove blacks from the voting booth and the jury box. The Court would not revisit this issue until *Norris v. Alabama* (1935), when it reaffirmed the holding in *Neal* that the absolute absence of blacks from the jury pools was unconstitutional discrimination. However, blacks did not begin to appear on southern juries in any significant numbers until the civil rights revolution of the 1960s and 1970s.

The Emergence of Another Race

Most issues of race and the Constitution in this period focused on the condition of African Americans. However, they were not the only group of nonwhites that faced discrimination and sought the protection of the Constitution. As noted in the introduction, the fate of American Indians under the Constitution is an epic and tragic story in its own right. Although any number of other ethnic groups might also be brought into this story of race and the Constitution, the story of the Chinese is particularly relevant to the history of race and the Constitution in this period.

Before the Civil War a significant number of Chinese immigrants came to the United States, mostly settling in California and Oregon. They faced blatant discrimination in those states. Like free blacks in the antebellum South, Asians in California and Oregon were not allowed to testify against whites. They were also segregated from public schools and other facilities both before and after the war. After the Civil War Congress amended the nation's naturalization laws to allow immigrants of African ancestry to become citizens, but did not extend this right to Asians. When Congress debated the Fourteenth Amendment some representatives from the West Coast tried to amend the citizenship clause to exclude Asians, but this move failed.

In 1882 Congress passed the Chinese Exclusion Act, the first significant restriction on immigration in American history. The law prohibited Chinese laborers from moving to the United States. The law, and subsequent amendments to it, had numerous exceptions and technical rules for Chinese entering the nation, or leaving the country and then returning. In *Chew Heong v. United States* (1884), also known as the Chinese Exclusion Cases, the Court, speaking through Justice Harlan, allowed Heong, a Chinese laborer, to re-enter the United States. While Heong was on a visit to China, Congress had passed an amendment to the 1882 law, requiring all Chinese living in the United States to obtain certain documents before they left the country, if they wanted to return. Justice Harlan wrote that Heong should not be excluded from the United States, because when he left the new law had not yet been passed and thus he could not have obtained the documents nor could he have known he would need them to return. Justice Stephen Field, who was from California and perhaps more hostile to Chinese immigrants than anyone else on the Court, argued that the Court should follow the law, as written, without regard for the unfairness of Heong's situation. While Heong was able to return to the United States, in *Chae Chan Ping v. United States* (1889) Field would write an opinion for a unanimous court holding that Congress was free to change the rules for returning to the nation, even if it meant that some Chinese aliens who had lived in the United States would never be able to return.

In the 1890s the Court tended to strictly follow the various exclusion laws, thus in *Lau Ow Bew* (1891) the Court allowed a Chinese man to return to the United States because he could prove he was a "merchant" and not a laborer, and the immigration restrictions only applied to laborers. But in *Fong Yue Ting v. United States* (1893) the Court held that Congress could not only exclude Chinese aliens, but also provide for their deportation. Similarly, in *Wong Wing v. United States* (1896) the Court ruled that the government could detain, arrest, and deport illegal Chinese aliens, but that they could not be sentenced to prison or have their property confiscated without a trial and full due process protections.

While generally unsympathetic to the claims of Chinese immigrants, in two cases involving Chinese, the Court interpreted the Fourteenth Amendment in ways that dramatically extended constitutional rights. In *Yick Wo v. Hopkins* (1886) the Court found that the San Francisco government had intentionally discriminated against Chinese when giving out licenses to operate laundries. A San Francisco ordinance required that all laundries be in brick buildings, unless they received an exemption. The city granted exemptions to every white except one who applied to operate a laundry in a wooden building. However, no exemptions were given to the more than two hundred Chinese who applied for licenses. Since building a brick laundry was prohibitively expensive, the law and this discriminatory application of it forced the Chinese to close their businesses. The Court held that the protections of the Fourteenth Amendment applied to "all persons" within the jurisdiction of the state, and not just to citizens. The city's ordinance was constitutional on its face, but its application violated the Fourteenth Amendment. This case did not end discrimination against the Chinese in California, but it provided a precedent that would later lead to an expansive notion of "equal protection" in the twentieth century.

Even more important than *Yick Wo* was the Court's decision in *United States v. Wong Kim Ark* (1898). Ark was born in the United States in 1873 and as a young adult he visited China. When he returned he was denied admission to the United States under the Chinese Exclusion Act. The Court ruled that under the Fourteenth Amendment *all* persons born in the United States, except the children of diplomats, were citizens of the United States. While a Chinese immigrant could not become naturalized, the children of immigrants born in the United States were in fact citizens of the United States and thus could not be denied reentry into the country.

The Supreme Court and the End of Civil Rights, 1883–96

While the Court was struggling with the status of Chinese immigrants and their children, much more of its energy was focused on the status of African Americans in post-Reconstruction America. In 1883 the Supreme Court decided three cases that dramatically set the tone for the future of race relations by restricting the Court's and Congress's ability to address the realities of racial discrimination on the ground. In *Pace v. Alabama* the Court upheld the two-year jail sentence of Tony Pace, a black man convicted of cohabitating with a white woman, Mary Cox. Pace argued that the Alabama statute violated the Fourteenth Amendment because if he had been white, or Cox had been black, they could not have been sent to jail for their offense. The Court held that this law did not discriminate on the basis of race, because it applied equally to whites who cohabitated with or tried to marry blacks, just as it applied to blacks who cohabitated with or tried to marry whites. In *United States v. Harris* the Court held that federal law could not be used to prosecute Harris and nineteen other men, who broke into a jail and beat up three black prisoners and murdered a fourth. The Court, over the objections of Justice Harlan, claimed that this racially motivated attack was "private" and that the Fourteenth Amendment only limited state action. Harlan, in dissent, argued that the purpose of the Thirteenth and Fourteenth Amendments was to protect the civil rights of the former slaves, and the federal law at issue in the case was constitutionally enacted.

Next the Court, in *The Civil Rights Cases* (1883), overturned most of the Civil Rights Act of 1875. Congress had passed this law to guarantee that blacks would have access to public accommodations, such as restaurants, theaters, and streetcars. Further developing the concept of "state action" it had articulated in *United States v. Harris*, the Court held that neither the Thirteenth nor the Fourteenth Amendment empowered Congress to prohibit segregation by private parties.[72] Although the Fourteenth Amendment had been drafted specifically to ensure freedmen's rights, Justice Bradley rejected the notion that Congress had affirmative powers under the amendment. Bradley argued that Congress could only act in response to state laws that discriminated on the basis of race. If a state enacted a law that restricted the rights of black citizens, Bradley believed Congress had the power to pass remedial legislation. But here Congress had acted to prevent private parties from discriminating, which the Court found was unconstitutional. Thus the Court severely restricted congressional power under the Fourteenth Amendment to protect the freedmen, leaving their fate in most cases to the states and their courts.

In a bitter dissent Justice Harlan argued that the Court had stripped the Fourteenth Amendment of its meaning. Harlan argued that Congress had the power to regulate public accommodations because they were "affected with a public interest."[73] He further argued that railroads, hotels, restaurants, theaters, and other public accommodations had always been regulated by the state. Thus, if the state failed to guarantee access to them, Congress was empowered to act. Harlan argued in his dissent that the licensing process for hotels, theaters, restaurants, or other public accommodations constituted sufficient state action for Congress to pass legislation guaranteeing equality. African American leaders bitterly reacted to this decision, understanding that the decision was the death knell for civil rights at the federal level. A number of northern states immediately passed their own civil rights laws, guaranteeing blacks access to hotels, restaurants, and public transportation, and in the next two decades northern state courts would enforce these laws. By 1900 almost every state outside of the South had adopted civil rights and equal accommodation laws. These laws protected the civil rights of blacks in the North, but at the time fewer than ten percent of all African Americans lived in the North. In the South blacks could not expect any legislation to guarantee equality.

Less than six months after the Court struck down the Civil Rights Act there was a final nineteenth-century civil rights victory for blacks. In *Ex parte Yarbrough* (1884) also known as the Ku Klux Klan Cases, the Court unanimously upheld the federal prosecution of members of the Ku Klux Klan in Georgia who had beaten a former slave who tried to vote. This case indicated that the Court still had some respect for the goals of the Civil War Amendments. However, even this position was short lived. Less than twenty years later, in *James v. Bowman* (1903) the Court would find that the law at issue in *Yarbrough* was unconstitutional.

The final end to Supreme Court support for civil rights came in the 1890s. In *Louisville, New Orleans & Texas Railway Co. v. Mississippi* (1890) the court upheld a Mississippi law that *required* all railroads in the state to provide "equal, but separate, accommodations for the white and colored races."[74] The Mississippi law seemed structurally identical to the Louisiana statute the Court had struck down on commerce clause grounds in *Hall v. DeCuir*. Both laws used race as a criterion for determining where passengers would be seated—the Louisiana law requiring integration and the Mississippi law requiring segregation. Both laws only applied within the state. In *Hall* the Court had found that requiring integration in Louisiana nevertheless burdened interstate commerce for ships that passed from one state to another. In *Louisville, New Orleans & Texas Railway Co. v. Mississippi*, however, the Court ignored this logic and held that because the Mississippi law applied only to that state, there was no burden on interstate commerce. Justice Harlan again dissented, pointing out that the ruling was obviously inconsistent with *Hall* and intellectually dishonest.

Hall had dealt only with the commerce clause. The plaintiff in the Mississippi case, the Louisville Railroad, did not raise the question of whether the Fourteenth Amendment prohibited state mandated segregation on the railroad, preferring to argue the case on commerce clause grounds. However, the Court soon addressed the question whether such legally mandated segregation violated the Fourteenth Amendment's guarantee of equal protection in the famous case of *Plessy v. Ferguson* (1896). There, the Court upheld a Louisiana law of 1890 that required railroads to provide "equal but separate accommodations for the white and colored races." In June 1892 Homer Adolph Plessy, who was one-eighth black, had refused to move to the "colored car" of an intrastate railroad, and was arrested. Plessy's act had been arranged by a group of New Orleans blacks who organized the Citizens Committee to Test the Constitutionality of the Separate Car Law. But their test failed. The Supreme Court agreed that the Fourteenth Amendment had been intended to establish an absolute equality of the races before the law, but then declared that "in the nature of things it could not have been intended to abolish distinctions based upon color, or to enforce social, as distinguished from political, equality, or a commingling of the two races unsatisfactory to either."[75] While never using the term "separate but equal," the Court's ruling approved the concept, and essentially gave the southern states a free hand to segregate blacks and whites throughout society, as long as the states claimed the separate facilities where "equal."

In one of the best-known dissents in the history of the Court, Justice Harlan warned that states could now impose criminal penalties on a citizen simply because he or she wished to use public highways and common carriers. Such legislation, Harlan argued was "inconsistent not only with equality of rights which pertains to citizenship, National and State, but with the personal liberty enjoyed by everyone within the United States."[76] The Kentucky-born Harlan condemned the Louisiana law as "conceived in hostility to, and enacted for the purpose of humiliating citizens of the United States of a particular race."[77] He believed this law, and others like it, defeated the purpose of the Civil War Amendments and would encourage racial hostility. Harlan argued that the "destinies of the two races ... are indissolubly linked together, and the interests of both require that the common government of all shall not permit the seeds of race hate to be planted under the sanction of law."[78]

Harlan acknowledged the power of white racism and the reality that whites were more powerful than blacks within American society. But he opposed the idea that the Constitution therefore allowed the white race to discriminate against blacks. He declared that in view of the Constitution, in the eye of the law, there is in this country no superior, dominant, ruling class of citizens. There is no caste here. Our Constitution is color-blind, and neither knows nor tolerates classes among citizens. In respect of civil rights, all citizens are equal before the law. The humblest is the peer of the most powerful. The law regards man as man, and takes no account of his surroundings or of his color when his civil rights as guaranteed by the supreme law of the land are involved. It is therefore to be regretted that this high tribunal, the final expositor of the fundamental law of the land, has reached the conclusion that it is competent for a State to regulate the enjoyment by citizens of their civil rights solely upon the basis of race.

Prophetically he predicted that "the judgment this day rendered will, in time, prove to be quite as pernicious as the decision made by this tribunal in the Dred Scott Case."[79]

Plessy has in fact gone down in history as one of the Court's worst decisions. The Court's acquiescence to segregation led to generations of southern blacks being denied access to equal schools, employment opportunities, and housing. By the eve of World War II virtually everything in the South would be rigidly segregated. All life in the South would be "separate" and nothing would be equal. *Plessy* would set the standard for race discrimination until the 1940s when the Court began to reject the idea of separate but equal. Social action, court decisions, presidential leadership, and legislation from the 1940s through the 1970s would finally dismantle segregation, and begin to redeem the promise of the Civil War Amendments.

Notes

1. There would be an excellent case for treating the Indian experience along with the black experience in this period, but space constraints make it impossible to do justice to both stories in a single pamphlet.

2. This pamphlet focuses mostly on the how the Constitution affected African Americans from the founding to the early twentieth century. Issues of race and the Constitution also affected Asians, who began to arrive in the late 1840s. Space does not allow for a complete investigation of Asian Americans and the Constitution in the nineteenth century, but I briefly discuss this experience in part 5 of this book.

3. The word "slave" also appears in the Fourteenth Amendment: "But neither the United States nor any State shall assume or pay any debt or obligation incurred in aid of insurrection or rebellion against the United States, or any claim for the loss or emancipation of any slave." Amend. XIV, Sec. 4.

4. Max Farrand, ed., *The Records of the Federal Convention of 1787* (New Haven: Yale University Press, 1966), 1:486; 2:10; 2:32; 2:56–57, 2:221–22; 2:371; 1:605.

5. During the debates over ratification many anti-federalists in the North noted the inherent dishonesty in the document's language. Thus, an anonymous author in Connecticut asked why the slave trade provision "should be couched in this blind mysterious form of words, unless to avoid using the word Negroes, I must leave to those that drew it to explain." He concluded that this clause was a sufficient reason to oppose the entire Constitution. "Letter from Massachusetts," *Connecticut Journal*, October 24, 1787, in Merrill Jensen, ed., *Documentary History of the Ratification of the Constitution* (Madison, State Historical Society of Wisconsin, 1976), 3:378–79. Similarly, in campaigning against the Constitution, the Connecticut politician Benjamin Gale attacked the "artful language they use to cover their meaning" in the slave trade provision. He asked: "Why all this sly cunning and artful mode of expression unless to cover from your observation and notice that Negroes was intended by the word persons ... lest it should frighten people who may have some tender feelings and a just sense of the rights of human nature." Benjamin Gale, "Address at the Constitutional Convention" (November 12, 1787), in Jensen, *Documentary History*, 424.

6. Farrand, *Records*, 1:561.

7. Farrand, *Records*, 2:425.

8. Jonathan Elliot, ed., *The Debates in the Several State Conventions on the Adoption of the Federal Constitution*, 5 vols. (New York: Burt Franklin, 1987), 4:176.

9. Gouverneur Morris thought the tax provision of the three-fifths clause was meaningless, because it was "idle to suppose that the General Government can stretch its hand directly into the pockets of the people scattered over so vast a Country." Farrand, *Records*, 2:223.

10. On Jefferson and slavery, see generally Paul Finkelman, *Slavery and the Founders: Race and Liberty in the Age of Jefferson*, 2d ed. (Armonk, N.Y.: M.E. Sharpe, 2001).

11. William W. Freehling, "The Founding Fathers and Slavery," *American Historical Review* 77 (1972): 82.

12. Elliot, *Debates*, 4:286.

13. Don E. Fehrenbacher, *The Federal Government and Slavery* (1984), 6. Equally untenable is the claim of law professor Earl Maltz that "the Constitution ... took no position on the basic institution of slavery." Earl Maltz, "Slavery, Federalism, and the Structure of the Constitution," *American Journal of Legal History* 36 (1992): 468.

14. Elliot, *Debates*, 3:598 and 4:286.

15. "Letters from a Countryman from Duchess County" (January 22, 1788) and "Essays by Republicus" (March 12, 1788) in *The Complete Anti-Federalist*, ed. Herbert Storing (Chicago: University of Chicago Press, 1981), 6:62 and 5:169.

16. James Wilson, "Remarks at the Penn. Convention" (December 3, 1787), in Jensen, *Documentary History*, 2:499 (1976). See also Paul Finkelman, "The American Suppression of the African Slave Trade: Lessons on Legal Change, Social Policy, and Legislation," *Akron Law Review* 42 (2009): 434.

17. Thomas Jefferson, "Sixth Annual Message," December 2, 1806, in ed. James D. Richardson, *A Compilation of the Messages and Papers of the Presidents* (New York: Bureau of National Literature, 1897), 1:396: "An Act to prohibit the importation of slaves into any port or place within the jurisdiction of the United States, from and after the first day of January, in the year of our Lord one thousand eight hundred and eight," 9th Cong., 2nd Sess., Act XXII, Act of March 2, 1807, 2 Stat. 426.

---

18. *Adams v. Woods*, 6 U.S. (2 Cranch) 336, 338–39 (1805).

19. *The Antelope*, 23 U.S. (10 Wheat.) 66, 121–22 (1825).

20. *The Antelope*, 122–23.

21. *The Amistad*, 40 U.S. (15 Pet.) 518, 593 (1841).

22. *Fugitive Slave Act of Feb. 1, 1793*, 1 Stat. 302, 303.

23. For a full discussion of the background of his case the opinion, see Paul Finkelman, "Story Telling on the Supreme Court: *Prigg v. Pennsylvania* and Justice Joseph Story's Judicial Nationalism," *Supreme Court Review, 1994* (1995): 247–94.

24. At least one of Morgan's children was born in Pennsylvania and thus free under the laws of that state. If Morgan was actually free, then all of Maryland-born children were also free from birth.

25. Paul Finkelman, "John McLean: Moderate Abolitionist and Supreme Court Politician," *Vanderbilt Law Review* 62 (2009): 519–65.

26. The Supreme Court misspelled Sanford's name as Sandford, which is how it appeared in the case. Sanford had business interests in St. Louis, and as long as he kept Scott in Missouri (or any other slave state) Sanford could legally own him, even though he lived in a free state.

27. *Dred Scott v. Sandford*, 60 U.S. (19 How.) 393, 450 (1857).

28. U.S. Constitution, Art. IV, Sec. 3, Par. 2.

29. Under a federal act of 1790 only whites could become naturalized citizens. It is theoretically possible that the antebellum Congress might have allowed for the naturalization of immigrant blacks, but in reality it would have been impossible to pass such a law. It is also possible that the Court would have found it unconstitutional to allow for the naturalization of blacks on the grounds, as stated in *Dred Scott* that at the founding "citizenship ... was perfectly understood to be confined to the white race; and that they alone constituted the sovereignty in the Government." *Dred Scott*, 419–20.

30. *Dred Scott*, 403.

31. *Smith v. Turner* (*The Passenger Cases*), 48 U.S. (7 How.) 283, 482–83 (1849).

32. *Smith v. Turner*, 283.

33. *Dred Scott*, 405.

34. *Dred Scott*, 404–05.

35. Both papers quoted in Don E. Fehrenbacher, *The Dred Scott Case: Its Significance in American Law and Politics* (New York: Oxford University Press, 1978), 417. For extensive newspaper response to the case, see Paul Finkelman, *Dred Scott v. Sandford: A Brief History with Documents* (Boston: Bedford Books, 1995).

36. *Charleston Daily Courier*, March 9, 1857, quoted in Fehrenbacher, *Dred Scott Case*, 418; *Washington Union*, March 11, 1857, p. 2.

37. See Finkelman, *Slavery and the Founders*, chap. 1 and Paul Finkelman, "Was Dred Scott Correctly Decided? An 'Expert Report' For the Defendant," *Lewis & Clark Law Review* 12 (2008): 1219–52.

38. Frederick Douglass, *Two Speeches by Frederick Douglass* (Rochester: C.P. Dewey, 1857), reprinted in Paul Finkelman, *Dred Scott v. Sandford*, 169.

39. Abraham Lincoln, "Second Inaugural Address," March 4, 1865, in ed. Roy P. Basler, *The Collected Works of Abraham Lincoln* (New Brunswick: Rutgers University Press, 1953), 8:332.

40. Abraham Lincoln, "First Inaugural Address—Final Text," March 4, 1861, in Basler, *Collected Works*, 4:262–63.

41. Paul Finkelman, "Lincoln, Emancipation, and the Limits of Constitutional Change," *Supreme Court Review, 2008* (2009): 349, at 364–65.

42. Butler and Lincoln quoted in Finkelman, "Lincoln, Emancipation."

43. Abraham Lincoln, "Reply to Emancipation Memorial Presented by Chicago Christians of All Denominations," September 13, 1862, in Basler, *Collected Works*, 5:419–25 (quotation on 421). For further discussion of the evolution of Lincoln's thought on this, see Finkelman, "Lincoln, Emancipation."

44. "Reply to Emancipation Memorial," 5:419–25 [quotations at 423].

45. "Reply to Emancipation Memorial," 5:419–25 [quotations at 423 and 420].

46. David Dudley Cornish, *The Sable Arm: Negro Troops in the Union Army, 1861–1865* (New York: W.W. Norton, 1966). Lewis Douglass was a sergeant major in the 54th Massachusetts regiment. His younger brother Charles served in the 54th as well but then transferred to the 5th Massachusetts Cavalry, where he became the regiment's First Sergeant.

47. *Report of the Joint Committee on Reconstruction*, 39th Cong., Resolution and Report of the Committee (1st Sess. 1866), xiii, xvii, xviii.

48. *Report of the Joint Committee*, xvii, xviii.

49. Act of Nov. 24, 1865, ch. 6, 1865 Alabama Laws 90 ("[p]rotect[ing] Freedmen in Their Rights of Person and Property in this State"). Act of Nov. 25, 1865, ch. 4, 1865 Mississippi Laws 82 ("an Act for conferring Civil Rights on Freedmen, and for other purposes"). Relevant portions of this act are reprinted in Melvin I. Urofsky and Paul Finkelman, *Documents of American Constitutional and Legal History*, 3d ed. (New York: Oxford University Press, 2007), 1:488-495.

50. *Report of the Joint Committee*, Part IV: Florida, Louisiana, Texas 125.

51. *Report of the Joint Committee*, Part IV, 26; Part III: Georgia, Alabama, Mississippi, Arkansas, 85–86, 166.

52. James M. McPherson, *The Struggle for Equality: Abolitionists and the Negro in the Civil War and Reconstruction* (Princeton: Princeton University Press, 1964), 341.

53. Unless otherwise noted, all quotations in this section are from the *Report of the Joint Committee*. Specific citations to all these quotations can be found in Paul Finkelman, "The Historical Context of the Fourteenth Amendment," *Temple Political & Civil Rights Law Review* 13 (2004): 389–409.

54. Text of the 1866 act can be found in Urofsky and Finkelman, *Documents of American Constitutional and Legal History*, 1:495–99.

55. Xi Wang, *The Trial of Democracy: Black Suffrage and Northern Republicans, 1860–1910* (Athens: University of Georgia Press, 1997); Paul Finkelman, "Civil Rights in Historical Context: In Defense of Brown," *Harvard Law Review* 118 (2005): 973–1027.

56. *Dred Scott*, 419–420.

57. *Dred Scott*, 481.

58. *Dred Scott*, 407.

59. The citizenship provision also applies to the American-born children of undocumented aliens living in the United States today. Some opponents of this result have argued that the phrase "subject to the jurisdiction thereof" means that the American-born children of undocumented aliens are not citizens because their parents are not "subject to" the jurisdiction of the United States and the state in which they live. But, this phrase in fact refers to the children of diplomats who are not subject to American law, because they have diplomatic immunity.

60. *Slaughter-house Cases*, 83 U.S. 36, 77 (1873).

61. Incorporation uses technical language and complex analysis to reach the conclusion that the "due process" clause of the Fourteenth Amendment prohibits the states from denying anyone fundamental liberties and that those liberties can be found in some of the provisions of the Bill of Rights. Hence, since 1925 the Court has selectively, on a piecemeal basis, held that the limitations on the federal government found in the Bill of Rights are also limitations on what the states can do. Thus, for example, the First Amendment, which says "Congress shall make no law respecting an establishment of religion" has been incorporated against the states, so now through the Fourteenth Amendment and the First Amendment, the states "shall make no law ... ."

62. *Blyew v. U.S.*, 80 U.S. 581, 590, 593–94 (1871).

63. *Blyew v. U.S.*, 596–601.

64. *Slaughter-house Cases*, 78.

65. *Hall v. DeCuir*, 95 U.S. 485 (1877).

66. *Strauder v. West Virginia*, 100 U.S. 303, 305 (1879).

67. *Strauder v. West Virginia*, 304–06.

68. *Commonwealth of Virginia v. Rives*, 100 U.S. 313, 321 (1879).

69. *Ex parte Virginia*, 100 U.S. 339, 347–48 (1879).

70. *Neal v. State of Delaware*, 103 U.S. 370, 372 (1880).

71. *Neal v. State of Delaware*, 394.

72. *U.S. v. Harris*, 106 U.S. 629 (1883).

73. *The Civil Rights Cases*, 109 U.S. 3, 42 (1883).

74. *Louisville, New Orleans & Texas Ry. Co. v. Mississippi*, 133 U.S. 587, 588 (1890).

75. *Plessy v. Ferguson*, 163 U.S. 537, 544 (1896).

76. *Plessy v. Ferguson*, 555.

77. *Plessy v. Ferguson*, 563.

78. *Plessy v. Ferguson*, 560.

79. *Plessy v. Ferguson*, 559.

Suggestions for Further Reading

*C*onsiderable attention has been given to the role slavery played at the Constitutional Convention, the debates over slavery during the ratification process, and the language of the Constitution with regard to slavery, including the fact that the term "slavery" was not used in the Constitution. These issues are discussed in Donald L. Robinson's hugely comprehensive work, *Slavery in the Structure of American Politics, 1765–1820* (New York: Harcourt Brace Jovanovich, 1971). The debates at the Convention are detailed in Paul Finkelman, *Slavery and the Founders: Race and Liberty in the Age of Jefferson,* 2nd ed. (Armonk, N.Y.: M.E. Sharpe, 2001); William M. Wiecek, "The Witch at the Christening: Slavery and the Constitution's Origins," in *The Framing and Ratification of the Constitution,* ed. Leonard W. Levy and Dennis J. Mahoney (New York: Macmillan, 1987); and David Waldstreicher, *Slavery's Constitution: From Revolution to Ratification* (New York: Hill and Wang, 2009). The best primary sources for these issues are in Max Farrand, ed., *The Records of the Federal Convention of 1787* (New Haven: Yale University Press, 1966); Jonathan Elliot, ed., *The Debates in the Several State Conventions on the Adoption of the Federal Constitution* (1888), 5 vols. (New York: Burt Franklin, 1987); and the multivolume, ongoing project published by the Wisconsin Historical Society, *The Documentary History of the Ratification of the Constitution.* The best discussion of the antislavery analysis of the Constitution is William M. Wiecek, *The Sources of Antislavery Constitutionalism, 1760–1848* (Ithaca: Cornell University Press, 1977). An antebellum antislavery criticism of the Constitution is Wendell Phillips, *Can Abolitionists Vote or Take Office under the United States Constitution* (New York: American Anti-slavery Society, 1845).

The nonconstitutional law of slavery affected constitutional developments in many ways. The federal courts often had to consider local law. The leading book on the law of slavery is Thomas D. Morris, *Southern Slavery and the Law, 1619–1860* (Chapel Hill: University of North Carolina Press, 1996). Also important is Mark V. Tushnet, *The American Law of Slavery, 1810–1860: Considerations of Humanity and Interest* (Princeton: Princeton

University Press, 1981) and Paul Finkelman, ed., *Slavery and the Law* (Madison, Wisc.: Madison House, 1997). Important specialized studies of slavery and the law include Judith Kelleher Schafer, *Slavery, the Civil Law, and the Supreme Court of Louisiana* (Baton Rouge: Louisiana State University Press, 1994); Schafer, *Becoming Free, Remaining Free: Manumission and Enslavement in New Orleans, 1846–1862* (Baton Rouge: Louisiana State University Press, 2003); Philip J. Schwarz, *Slave Laws in Virginia* (Athens: University of Georgia Press, 1996); Mark V. Tushnet, *Slave Law in the American South:* State v. Mann *in History and Literature* (Lawrence: University of Kansas Press, 2003); Sally Green, "*State v. Mann* Exhumed," *University of North Carolina Law Review* 87 (2009): 701–55; and Bernie Jones, *Fathers of Conscience: Mixed Race Inheritance in the Antebellum South* (Athens: University of Georgia Press, 2009). Three contemporary treatises on the law of slavery are Jacob D. Wheeler, *A Practical Treatise on the Law of Slavery* (New York: Allan Pollack Jr., 1837); John Codman Hurd, *The Law of Freedom and Bondage in the United States*, 2 vols. (Boston: Little Brown, 1858 and 1862); and Thomas R.R. Cobb, *An Inquiry into the Law of Negro Slavery* (1858; repr., Athens: University of Georgia Press, 1999).

The social and political changes with respect to African Americans during this period had a substantial impact on the American Indians. For sources that discuss the colonial period to 1830 see James F. Brooks, ed., *Confounding the Color Line: The Indian-Black Experience in North America* (Lincoln: University of Nebraska Press, 2002) and James H. Merrell, "The Racial Education of the Catawba Indians," *Journal of Southern History* 50, no. 3 (August 1984): 363–84. For a discussion of American Indian experience from the antebellum era though the Civil War see Tim Alan Garrison, *The Legal Ideology of Removal: The Southern Judiciary and the Sovereignty of Native American Nations* (Athens: University of Georgia Press, 2002); Theda Perdue, *Slavery and the Evolution of the Cherokee Society, 1540–1866* (Knoxville: University of Tennessee Press, 1979); Daniel F. Littlefield Jr., *Africans and Seminoles: From Removal to Emancipation* (Westport, Conn.: Greenwood, 1978); and Littlefield, *Africans and Creeks: From the Colonial Period to the Civil War* (Westport, Conn.: Greenwood, 1979).

The African slave trade and associated cases are discussed in Paul Finkelman, ed., *Articles on American Slavery,* vol. 2, *The Slave Trade and Migration* (New York: Garland Publishing, 1989) and Peter Duignan and Clarence Clendenen, *The United States and the African Slave Trade, 1619–1862* (Stanford, Calif.: Stanford University Press, 1963). The most recent study of the laws ending the trade is Paul Finkelman, "Regulating the African Slave Trade," *Civil War History* 54 (2008): 379–405. For a more comprehensive discussion of *The Antelope* and its relation to the slave trade see John T. Noonan Jr., *The Antelope: The Ordeal of the Recaptured Africans in the Administration of James Monroe and John Quincy Adams* (Berkeley: University of California Press, 1977). For the *Amistad* see Howard Jones, *Mutiny on the Amistad: The Saga of a Slave Revolt and Its Impact on American Abolition, Law, and Diplomacy* (New York: Oxford University Press, 1987).

The fugitive slave laws and their resulting litigation have been examined in a multitude of works. See Stanley Campbell, *The Slave Catchers: Enforcement of the Fugitive Slave Law, 1850–1860* (Chapel Hill: University of North Carolina); Paul Finkelman, "Fugitive Slaves, Midwestern Racial Tolerance, and the Value of 'Justice Delayed,'" *Iowa Law Review* 78 (1992): 89–141; Finkelman, *Slavery in the Courtroom* (Washington, D.C.: Library of Congress, 1985); Carol Wilson, *Freedom at Risk: The Kidnapping of Free Blacks in America, 1780–1865* (Lexington: University of Kentucky Press, 1994); and H. Robert Baker, *The Rescue of Joshua Glover: A Fugitive Slave, The Constitution, and the Coming of the Civil War* (Athens: Ohio University Press, 2006). For more specifically on the Supreme Court case of *Prigg v. Pennsylvania* see Paul Finkelman, "Sorting out *Prigg v. Pennsylvania*," *Rutgers Law Journal* 24 (1993): 605–65 and "Story Telling on the Supreme Court: *Prigg v. Pennsylvania* and Justice Joseph Story's Judicial Nationalism," *Supreme Court Review, 1994* (1995): 247–94.

The Northwest Ordinance passed in 1787 and its connection to the development of the Constitution can be found in David O. Stewart, *The Summer of 1787: The Men Who Invented the Constitution* (New York: Simon & Schuster, 2007); Paul Finkelman, *Slavery and the Founders: Race and Liberty in the Age of Jefferson*, 2d ed. (Armonk, N.Y.: M.E. Sharpe, 2001); and James Simeone, *Democracy and Slavery in Frontier Illinois: The Bottomland Republic* (DeKalb: Northern Illinois University Press, 2000). On the problem of interstate transit and slavery see Paul Finkelman, *An Imperfect Union: Slavery, Federalism, and Comity* (Chapel Hill: University of North Carolina Press, 1981).

The Compromise of 1820, also known as the Missouri Compromise, and its related controversies is discussed in Robert Forbes, *The Missouri Compromise and Its Aftermath: Slavery and the Meaning of America* (Chapel Hill: University of North Carolina Press, 2007). This updates the classic work on the subject, Glover Moore, *The Missouri Controversy, 1819–1821* (Gloucester, Mass.: Peter Smith, 1967).

The Crisis of the 1850s has attracted many leading scholars and led to some of the best scholarship on the antebellum period. The best place to start for a discussion of the Compromise of 1850 is David M. Potter's Pulitzer Prize-winning *The Impending Crisis 1848–1861,* ed. and comp. by Don E. Fehrenbacher (New York: Harper and Row, 1976). The compromise is placed in a much larger perspective in William W. Freehling, *The Road to Disunion: Secessionists at Bay, 1776–1854* (New York: Oxford University Press, 1990). Michael F. Holt, *The Political Crisis of the 1850s* (New York: John Wiley, 1978) also puts the compromise in perspective. Holman Hamilton, *Prologue to Conflict: The Crisis and Compromise of 1850* (Lexington: University of Kentucky Press, 1964) details the debates over the compromise. On the politics of the compromise at the presidential level, see Paul Finkelman, *Millard Fillmore* (New York: Times Books, 2011). See also John C. Waugh, *On the Brink of Civil War: The Compromise of 1850 and How it Changed the Course of American History* (Wilmington, Del.: Scholarly Resources, 2003).

The landmark case of *Dred Scott v. Sandford* (1857) had a substantial impact American jurisprudence. The most important work is Don E. Fehrenbacher, *The Dred Scott Case: Its Significance in American Law and Politics* (New York: Oxford University Press, 1978), which won the Pulitzer Prize. Walter Ehrlich, *They Had No Rights: Dred Scott's Struggle for Freedom* (Westport, Conn.: Greenwood Press, 1979) provides valuable information on the details of the case, especially in Missouri. Paul Finkelman, *Dred Scott v. Sandford: A Brief History* (Boston: Bedford Books, 1995) provides a documentary history of the case. *Dred Scott's* sesquicentennial coincided with an outpouring of work on the case, including Mark Graber, *Dred Scott and the Problem of Constitutional Evil* (New York: Cambridge University Press, 2006); Austin Allen, *The Origins of the Dred Scott Case: Jacksonian Jurisprudence and the Supreme Court, 1837–1857* (Athens: University of Georgia Press, 2006); David T. Konig, Paul Finkelman, and Christopher A. Bracey, eds., *The Dred Scott Case: Historical and Contemporary Perspectives on Race and Law* (Athens: Ohio University Press, 2010); "Symposium: 150th Anniversary of the *Dred Scott* Decision," *Chicago Kent Law Review* 82 (2007): 3–458 (symposium editors Paul Finkelman, Jack M. Balkin, and Sanford Levinson); and Earl M. Maltz, *Dred Scott and the Politics of Slavery* (Lawrence: University Press of Kansas, 2007). In 2007 Harvard Law School had a moot court re-argument of *Dred Scott* that led to Paul Finkelman, "Was Dred Scott Correctly Decided? An 'Expert Report' For the Defendant," *Lewis & Clark Law Review* 12 (2008): 1219–52.

The Civil War led to profound changes in both the Constitution and the United States as a nation. See David Herbert Donald, Jean Harvey Baker, and Michael F. Holt, *The Civil War and Reconstruction* (New York: Norton, 2001); Joseph T. Glatthaar, *Forged in Battle: The Civil War Alliance of Black Soldiers and White Officers* (New York: Free Press, 1990); James M. McPherson, *Battle Cry of Freedom: The Civil War Era* (New York: Oxford University Press, 1988); and McPherson, *The Struggle for Equality: Abolitionists and the Negro in the Civil War and Reconstruction* (Princeton: Princeton University Press, 1964). See Catherine Clinton and Nina Silber, eds., *Divided Houses: Gender and the Civil War* (New York: Oxford University Press, 1992) for an exploration of the impact of the Civil War on gender relations during reconstruction. For information on Frederick Douglass and his connection to the Civil War see David W. Blight, *Frederick Douglass' Civil War: Keeping Faith in Jubilee* (Baton Rouge: Louisiana State University Press, 1989).

The Emancipation Proclamation freed millions of slaves in the South, although it took the U.S. Army to effectuate this freedom. See LaWanda Cox, *Lincoln and Black Freedom: A Study in Presidential Leadership* (Columbia: University of South Carolina Press, 1981); John Hope Franklin, *The Emancipation Proclamation* (Garden City, N.Y.: Doubleday, 1963); Michael P. Johnson, ed., *Abraham Lincoln, Slavery, and the Civil War: Selected Writings and Speeches* (Boston: Bedford/St. Martin's, 2001); and Leon F. Litwack, *Been in the Storm So Long: The Aftermath of Slavery* (New York: Knopf, 1979). For more specifically on the Lincoln administration, the Emancipation Proclamation, and its impact on race and the Constitution see Paul Finkelman, "Lincoln, Emancipation, and the Limits of Constitutional Change," *Supreme Court Review, 2008* (2009): 364–65; Eric Foner, ed., *Our Lincoln: New Perspectives on Lincoln and His World* (New York: W.W. Norton, 2008); and William A. Blair and Karen Fisher Younger, eds., *Lincoln's Proclamation: Race, Place, and the Paradoxes of Emancipation* (Chapel Hill: University of North Carolina Press, 2009).

The end of the Civil War led to discussions regarding American race relations. For more on the jurisprudence during this period and particularly more on the Thirteenth and Fourteenth Amendments see Harold M. Hyman and William M. Wiecek, *Equal Justice under Law: Constitutional Development, 1835–1875* (New York: Harper and Row, 1982) and Jacobus tenBroek, *The Antislavery Origins of the Fourteenth Amendment* (Berkeley: University of California Press, 1951). For more on the Fifteenth Amendment and the right to vote see William Gillette, *The Right to Vote: Politics and the Passage of the Fifteenth Amendment* (Baltimore: Johns Hopkins University Press, 1965).

For more on the impact of the Civil Rights Act of 1866 see Donald G. Nieman, *Promises to Keep: African Americans and the Constitutional Order, 1776 to the Present* (New York: Oxford University Press, 1991). A discussion of post-Civil War race relations including a discussion of southern violence, the southern black codes, and constitutions passed in 1865 and 1866 can be found in James M. McPherson, *The Struggle for Equality: Abolitionists and the Negro in the Civil War and Reconstruction* (Princeton: Princeton University Press, 1964).

For more on race relations see John Hope Franklin, *Reconstruction: After the Civil War* (Chicago: University of Chicago Press, 1961); Eric Foner, *Reconstruction: America's Unfinished Revolution 1863–1877* (New York: Harper and Rowe, 1988); David J. Libby, *Slavery and Frontier Mississippi, 1720–1835* (Jackson: University of Mississippi Press, 2004); and Vernon Lane Wharton, *The Negro in Mississippi, 1865–1890* (Chapel Hill: University of North Carolina Press, 1947).

The Supreme Court's interpretation of the Fourteenth Amendment as addressed in the *Slaughter-House Cases* (1873) is analyzed in William E. Nelson, *The Fourteenth Amendment: From Political Principle to Judicial Doctrine* (Cambridge: Harvard University Press, 1988); Ronald M. Labbe and Jonathan Lurie, *The Slaughterhouse Cases: Regulation, Reconstruction, and the Fourteenth Amendment* (Lawrence: University Press of Kansas, 2003); and Loren Beth, "The Slaughter-House Cases—Revisited," *Louisiana Law Review* 23 (1963): 487–505. The role of Justice Miller in writing the opinion in this case is set out in Michael A. Ross, *Justice of Shattered Dreams: Samuel Freeman Miller and the Supreme Court during the Civil War Era* (Baton Rouge: Louisiana State University Press, 2003).

After the Civil War, the Civil Rights Act of 1875 was created to facilitate the reconstruction of race relations. See Eric Foner and Olivia Mahoney, *America's Reconstruction: People and Politics after the Civil War* (New York: HarperPerennial, 1995); Kirt H. Wilson, *The Reconstruction Desegregation Debate: The Politics of Equality and the Rhetoric of Place, 1870–1875* (East Lansing: Michigan State University Press, 2002); and Bertram Wyatt-Brown, "The Civil Rights Act of 1875," *Western Political Quarterly* 18, no. 4 (December 1965): 763–65.

The Supreme Court's decisions in cases concerning racial violence have been discussed by a number of scholars. See Robert J. Kaczorowski, *The Politics of Judicial Interpretation: The Federal Courts, Department of Justice and Civil Rights, 1866–1876* (Dobbs Ferry, N.Y.: Oceana Publications,

1985); Xi Wang, *The Trial of Democracy: Black Suffrage and Northern Republicans, 1860–1910* (Athens: University of Georgia Press, 1997); James M. McPherson, *The Struggle for Equality: Abolitionists and the Negro in the Civil War and Reconstruction* (Princeton: Princeton University Press, 1964); and George C. Rable, *But There Was No Peace: The Role of Violence in the Politics of Reconstruction* (Athens: University of Georgia Press, 1964).

For more specifically on the Ku Klux Klan and related litigation see Lou Falkner Williams, *The Great South Carolina Ku Klux Klan Trials, 1871–1872* (Athens: University of Georgia Press 1996) and James Michael Martinez, *Carpetbaggers, Cavalry, and the Ku Klux Klan: Exposing the Invisible Empire during Reconstruction* (Rowman & Littlefield Publishers, 2007).

The problem of segregation and the Court has been extensively examined. *Plessy v. Ferguson*, the most famous segregation case, is discussed in Charles A. Lofgren, *The Plessy Case: A Legal-Historical Interpretation* (New York: Oxford University Press, 1987). Also see Pauli Murray, ed. and comp., *State Laws on Race and Color* (Cincinnati: Women's Division of Christian Service, 1952; repr., Athens: University of Georgia Press, 1997), which provides the best summary of segregation laws. Books connecting the late nineteenth century to the twentieth century include Richard Kluger, *Simple Justice* (New York: Knopf, 1975); C. Vann Woodward, *The Strange Career of Jim* Crow, 3d rev. ed. (New York: Oxford University Press, 1989); and Catherine A. Barnes, *Journey from Jim Crow: The Desegregation of Southern Transit* (New York: Columbia University Press, 1983).

The permissible uses of race in empanelling juries were hotly disputed during this period. See Donald G. Nieman, *Promises to Keep: African Americans and the Constitutional Order, 1776 to the Present* (New York: Oxford University Press, 1991); Benno C. Schmidt Jr., "Juries, Jurisdiction, and Race Discrimination: The Lost Promise of *Strauder v. West Virginia*," *Texas Law Review* 61 (1983): 1401–99; and Douglas Colbert, "Challenging the Challenge: Thirteenth Amendment as a Prohibition Against the Racial Use of Preemptory Challenges," *Cornell Law Review* 76 (1990): 1.

The story of the Chinese is particularly relevant to the history of race and the Constitution. See Lucy E. Salyer, *Laws Harsh as Tigers: Chinese Immigrants and the Shaping of Modern Immigration Law* (Chapel Hill: University of North Carolina Press, 1995); Hyung-Chan Kim, *A Legal History of Asian Americans 1790–1990* (Westport Conn.: Greenwood Press, 1994); Charles J. McClain, *In Search of Equality: The Chinese Struggle against Discrimination in Nineteenth-Century America* (Berkeley: University of California

Press, 1994); and Stuart Creighton Miller, *The Unwelcome Immigrant: The American Image of the Chinese, 1785–1882* (Berkeley: University of California Press, 1969). On the relationship between segregation of blacks and discrimination against Chinese, see Gabriel J. Chin, "The *Plessy* Myth: Justice Harlan and the Chinese Cases," *Iowa Law Review* 82 (1996): 151. For a discussion of the definition of race in the context of immigration, see Ian F. Haney Lopez, *White by Law: The Legal Construction of Race* (New York: NYU Press, 1996). For a different view of *Yick Wo v. Hopkins*, see Gabriel J. Chin, "Unexplainable on Grounds of Race: Doubts about *Yick Wo*," *University of Illinois Law Review*, 2008 (2008): 1359.

Between 1883 and 1896 the Supreme Court decided several cases that set the tone for the future of race relations by restricting the Court's and Congress's ability to address the realities of racial discrimination. See Pauli Murray, ed. and comp., *States' Laws on Race and Color* (Cincinnati: Women's Division of Christian Service, 1952; repr., Athens: University of Georgia Press, 1997); and C. Vann Woodward, *The Strange Career of Jim Crow*, 3d rev. ed. (New York: Oxford University Press, 1989); J. David Hoeveler Jr., "Reconstruction and the Federal Courts: The Civil Rights Act of 1875," *History* 31 (1969): 604; and John A. Scott, "Justice Bradley's Evolving Concept of the Fourteenth Amendment from the Slaughterhouse Cases to the Civil Rights Cases," *Rutgers Law Review* 25 (1971): 552.

For discussion on *Pace v. Alabama*, see R. Carter Pittman, "The Fourteenth Amendment: Its Intended Effect on Anti-Miscegenation Laws," *North Carolina Law Review* 43 (1964) 92; Peter Wallenstein, "Race, Marriage, and the Law of Freedom: Alabama and Virginia, 1860s–1960s," *Chicago-Kent Law Review* 70 (1994): 371; Peter Wallenstein, *Tell the Court I Love My Wife: Race, Marriage, and Law—An American History* (New York: Palgrave Macmillan, 2002); and Peggy Pascoe, *What Comes Naturally: Miscegenation Law and the Making of Race in America* (New York: Oxford University Press, 2009).